DRAWN TO THE LIGHT

Drawn to the Light

Poems and Essays

CARROLL E. ARKEMA

RESOURCE *Publications* • Eugene, Oregon

DRAWN TO THE LIGHT
Poems and Essays

Copyright © 2019 Carroll E. Arkema. All rights reserved. Except for brief quotations in critical publications or reviews, no part of this book may be reproduced in any manner without prior written permission from the publisher. Write: Permissions, Wipf and Stock Publishers, 199 W. 8th Ave., Suite 3, Eugene, OR 97401.

Resource Publications
An Imprint of Wipf and Stock Publishers
199 W. 8th Ave., Suite 3
Eugene, OR 97401

www.wipfandstock.com

PAPERBACK ISBN: 978-1-5326-9168-3
HARDCOVER ISBN: 978-1-5326-9169-0
EBOOK ISBN: 978-1-5326-9170-6

Manufactured in the U.S.A.   JULY 15, 2019

"A Spiritual Teacher," is reprinted from Reflective Practice: Formation and Supervision in Ministry. Vol. 36, 2016, pp. 118-125.

"One Thing She Said, One Thing She Did," is reprinted from Reflective Practice: Formation and Supervision in Ministry. Vol 39, 2019, pp. 185-190.

Scripture quotations noted The Holy Bible (NRSV) are taken from the New Revised Standard Version Bible, copyright 1989, Division of Christian Education of the National Council of Churches of Christ in the United States of America. Used by permission. All rights reserved.

Dedicated to

Dan R. Bottorff, D. Min.

who has invited me
into the "limelight"
of public Readings of my poems
in various venues
and has been
a faithful friend
for forty years!

Contents

Author's Preface / ix
Acknowledgements / xiii

Childhood / 1
    Grandma's Kitchen / 1
    One Legacy of Trauma / 4
    Transfiguration at Grandma's Funeral / 7

Youth / 10
    Muscles / 10
    Fire in Sully, Iowa, 1967 / 12
    Oases in the Desert of Dad / 14

Young Adulthood: My Vocational Choice / 30
    Willis P. DeBoer / 30
    Afraid to Preach / 34

Formation as a Pastor / 40
    One Thing She Said, One Thing She Did / 40
    Supervising the Angry Student/Supervisee / 47

Pastoral Psychotherapy / 61
    Words Create Self and World / 61
    What a Therapist Does / 72
    A Spiritual Teacher / 74
    My Mother's Pain / 84
    Disappearing No More / 89

Later Adulthood / 105
    How I Got to Know my Dad / 105
    Love Travel / 107

Reflections on Art, Darkness, and Light / 108
    The Human Position: Made in the Image of God / 108
    Velasquez' Adoration of the Magi / 128
    Rembrandt's Judas / 134
    Ask Anything / 147
    The Abyss / 152
    What's In a Face? / 161
    Moonlight Glimmer / 185

Bibliography / 187

Author's Preface

A COUPLE OF THEMES emerged as I thought about putting together this my third book: first, my gradual emergence from hiding my "light"—my gifts and talents; and second, my discovering as I let it shine that the light in me was a gift of Divine Life and Light which illumines my path and can illuminate others' paths too and encourage them to let their light shine. I have become more alive and creative, and though I at times doubt the value of what I have to say, more often I understand more fully the statement in the Gospel of John[1] that "the light shines in the darkness, and the darkness did not overcome it."

One way of describing my emergence is that I've been birthed out of hiding, and that I've been gradually coming out of hiding ever since I was born. My mother delivered me into this world biologically, but very early I hid my soul: my soul was too frightened to feel safe in the world till much later. Up until I was seven or eight, my Dad would sometimes hit me as punishment until I'd learned to hide everything except compliance. I lived two lives—one intertwined with the other, the public and the private. I kept my soul hidden with God, but it was the deep source of my life, literally and figuratively.

My soul lived, I see now, in words—it dwelt in words; firstly, the words of the Bible, and secondly, the words of Literature. The Bible is the first book I heard read—by my Dad after meals; by the minister in church; and Bible stories read to my two brothers and me by my mother at bedtime. These were stories of lives lived in the presence of God, in relationship with God. I resonated with them in a way I didn't fully understand until much later.

---

1. The Holy Bible NRSV, John 1:5.

In my Junior High School years, I loved sermons based on Old Testament/Hebrew Bible stories: for example, a series about Joseph—his being favored by his father, betrayed by his brothers, tempted sexually but remaining chaste, then coming into his own due to his interpretations of dreams for the Pharoah—which I understood as being due to his connection to, and discernment of, divine activity in the world. I lived my hidden life—the life of my soul—through these and other biblical stories

At some point in High School, I had the thought that I wanted to become a minister. I admired the Religion teacher—who was also a Preacher—in my (private Christian) high school. As a sophomore in College, I decided to pursue the ministry; I majored in English—words again—and minored in Religion—biblical words again.

I pursued, thankfully, the best education my world had to offer: went to Calvin College and Princeton Theological Seminary; graduated; but was still afraid to share my soul with the world—even in the guise/cloak of a Pastor. After avoiding actual parish ministry for two years—during which time I got into psychotherapy and undertook a year of supervised ministry which helped me begin to integrate my private hidden soul into a vocation—I entered parish ministry. Within two years, I realized I wanted to do therapy—be a therapist: I wanted to as be helpful as my first therapist had been to me: he helped me to feel nonjudgmentally heard and accepted. I acquired training to be a psychotherapist, and increasingly over the next twenty-five years let my soul come out of hiding.

However, I continued to be aware of a certain emptiness within myself—an anxiety about the ever-lurking Void or Nothingness in life: life's soullessness, I'd say in hindsight.

I'd been with three therapists over those twenty-five years—all helpful in various ways. But still the anxiety lurked. I told a best friend about it: and I was surprised when he said he felt it too at times, and he suggested that we talk by phone every other week to help each other with this. We talked like this for almost two years.

Author's Preface

During that time, I didn't fully realize that these talks weren't getting at the heart of the matter, until our conversation the day after the 2008 Presidential election. I was expressing to him my doubts about Barack Obama. We were both Democrats, but I was troubled by some of Obama's proposed policies. I think that I expressed myself in an over-determined way that was derived from my underlying emptiness and negativity. He got angry and hung up the phone on me. His wife had just been diagnosed with serious cancer, and I think my negativity was more than he could take. But at the time, I was devastated: I felt panicky, abandoned, cut off, and helpless—desperately alone in the world, and also angry at his not talking things through.

I went for a walk in Central Park during a midday break in my schedule on that Wednesday and on successive Wednesdays. Over the course of the next few weeks, something began happening in a way I still don't fully understand: I began to think of writing poetry. The first line of my first poem—which I later titled "Panic"—began to take shape in my head. I toyed with the words of that first line, over and over: the words began to be accompanied by a certain rhythm, which helped me choose precisely the words which fit best: "through rolling time's interstices." I had never used the word "interstices" before; I had to look it up in the dictionary. That line somehow anchored me for a few weeks. I see now that it began to fill the emptiness, the loneliness.

By writing, I realize now that I was accompanying myself—understanding myself in a way that no one else could do quite as well. And I felt subliminally accompanied by what I would now call the Spirit. Gradually, the following lines took shape: "Through rolling Time's interstices,/which I thought neat and tightly sewn,/ sheer panic pops—or is it Void?—/and rips a ragged hole so large/ that Panic's all there is."

The words to the rest of the poem continued to come over the next few weeks: they traced my journey—expressed the journey that my soul had been on all along. The poem captured the feelings of the Void, but the further words which came to me as I continued to write, helped me to realize that I experience a Divine Presence which keeps me alive and upholds me even in the midst of the Void. It was like my soul was bursting forth and suddenly I was integrating a bible verse that had intrigued, puzzled, and thrilled me for years: suddenly now it made sense: "Enoch walked with God; then he was no more, for God took him."[2] Then with striking clarity, these words came to me: "Void's redefined/ as life with God forevermore." That poem "Panic," is the first poem in my first book Beyond Me: Poems about Spirit in Scripture, Psychotherapy, and Life.

I was writing words that came to me even before they seemed logical or made sense. But I wrote them, and later I realized that they captured all that's involved in one's relationship with God: "I, but not I, but God in me"; being and nonbeing; life and death.

Something compelled me to submit the poem to the Journal of Religion and Health, and the Editor excitedly accepted it for publication! I was thrilled, felt affirmed and encouraged. I kept writing, and he accepted and published my next three poems as well!

My life was re-inspired—my private life, my hidden soul, burst forth. In summarizing my life till now: I was in-spired—breathed into—by the Spirit's breath at biological birth, then re-inspired by the Spirit's creativity through my soul as expressed in the form of words—both in doing talk-therapy and in writing.

I've arranged the Contents of the book in the chronological order of my life, with most of the poems and essays marking experiences which helped me emerge from hiding and grow towards the light. The final section expresses my later experiences of darkness and light and my responses to works by other artists who deal with darkness and light.

I wrote that first poem eleven years ago, at age fifty-nine, and my life has been re-inspired in a much fuller, richer, more creative way ever since. I feel more alive and "out there" than ever before.

I hope that this book reminds Readers of those persons and experiences in their own lives which drew them towards the Light outside, and inside, themselves and helped them be more alive.

2. Ibid., Genesis 5:24.

Acknowledgements

WHEN I TRY TO express the depth of my gratitude to all those who have supported me in putting together this book, I find myself thinking of that verse in "Hebrews": ". . . since we are surrounded by so great a cloud of witnesses . . ."[1]

I have been surrounded by people who have sometimes witnessed the Holy Spirit's presence and inspiration in my writing, and especially when I'm reading my poems aloud. I have continually and consistently been affirmed and encouraged beyond what I ever imagined could happen, which has continued to inspire me to write more and read more, and so on and on.

Thanks first of all to everyone at Wipf and Stock Publishers—especially Matt Wimer, who has been my primary contact person—who have believed in me for the third time now, and have been supportive, gracious, and professional in the publication process.

Thanks to Dan Bottorff—to whom I have dedicated this book—for his forty-year-long friendship and collegiality; to Roger Plantikow, who during the course of our forty-two-year relationship has moved from being my Supervisor to Instructor to Mentor to Colleague, and now Friend for the last twenty years.

Thanks next to Mairead Stack—my Life Partner for the last twenty-two years—for her constant love and responses to my writing, and for adding immeasurable richness to my life.

Thanks to my brother Ken, who has stunned me with his depth of response to my poems ever since I first started writing twelve years ago. He drove hundreds of miles between snow storms from Iowa to meet me at Villa Maria Retreat Center in eastern Pennsylvania to spend an entire weekend discussing each poem in

1. The Holy Bible NRSV, Hebrews 12:1a.

my first book—at a depth of spirituality that anticipated, and has not been surpassed, by other discussions of my poems.

My brother Dean has also been encouraging and honest in his responses to my writing, and Ken and Dean's wives, Pat and Gayle, respectively, have been excited and affirming of my writing and being published.

The Rev. Alan Arkema, my paternal uncle, has shared intimately and movingly of the Holy Spirit's healing, guiding, and sustaining presence throughout his life—as mediated through his mother; colleagues who lovingly challenged him; and his study of the Bible. His immediate appreciation of my writing was thrilling, and he has successfully pursued his own writing.

Several Pastoral Psychotherapy colleagues have been moved by my poems and have been strongly affirming and encouraging. Charles Mayer was the first to call me a Poet, and he and Leslye Noyes have been colleagues for over ten years now in our bimonthly meetings, helping me realize the spiritual power in my poetry. Other colleagues who have responded at this depth are Mary and Tim Barrett, Sue Bottorff, Thea Crites, Ron Dieter, Marianne Farrin, John Karl, Bill Manseau, John Mokkosian, Gardner Perry, Margaret (Peg) Pipchick, Doug Ronsheim, Scott Sullender, S. Bruce Wagner, Jim Wildman (a lawyer), Tim Wildman, and Tom Willingham. Robert C. Dykstra, Professor of Pastoral Theology at Princeton Theological Seminary, has been congratulatory and encouraging.

Dan Bottorff was the first person to invite me to read my poetry aloud. He invited me twice to groups at his church, as also did the Rev. Todd Shumpert once at the church he was serving. These public Readings were initially daunting but ultimately amazing and even at times transporting experiences for me—as an introverted person—to no longer hide my light, but instead to let it shine!

Roger Plantikow and the Rev. Sarah Lee invited me to read a poem as part of their Sunday Worship Service, and then to read more poems during lunch after worship. The response and discussion thrilled and amazed me!

Acknowledgements

Chaplain Nancy Truscott and O. Bonnie Babson invited me to read at Crane's Mill (Retirement Community) for a Memorial Service. Then John Mokkosian and Ron Dieter invited and facilitated my Readings at three worship services at the annual Eastern and Northeastern Regional conference of the American Association of Pastoral Counselors in October, 2018.

Earlier that year, in April, 2018, Mary De Jong and Bob Zylstra invited me to read at nine different venues over ten days near my hometown in Pella, Iowa, where I had gone to high school and graduated in 1966. They spent hours sponsoring and arranging these Readings at churches, two Bereavement Groups (at a hospice and a funeral home), and at a local Clergy Ministerium. The principal at Pella Christian High, Dan Van Kooten, arranged for me to read to a Senior High Literature Class taught by Noreen Vander Wal, who was warmly hospitable. During that ten-day Reading Tour, my Elementary School classmate Barb Kopaska hosted Mairead and me for a Reading to my elementary school alums at her home, which was attended by half of my sixteen fellow alums and some of their spouses.

At each and every one of these Readings, I've been astounded, deeply moved, enriched, and enlightened by the responses which my poems elicit from the hearers.

A cloud of witnesses, indeed, who respond to my poems and nurture me at all levels of depth, and encourage me to continue writing and doing Readings.

I hope the readers of this book find the poems and essays meaningful and inspiring, and that they are stimulated to remember their own life-changing experiences and memories.

I can't mention them by name (for reasons of confidentiality), but several of my Pastoral Psychotherapy patients have inspired poems about our work together, and I continue to be thrilled and humbled by the way that the Spirit heals and transforms a person's life if that person is open to the process. It is indeed "a fearful thing to fall into the hands of the living God,"[2] but the more one accepts

---

2. Ibid., 10:31.

that "living God" within oneself, words can scarcely express the peace, trust, and joy that ensues.

Thanks to all these people whom I've named and more whom I've no doubt forgotten to mention, who have supported and inspired me in the two mutually enhancing roles of my Calling: Pastoral Psychotherapist and Poet. Thanks mostly to the Living God, who, through Jesus, says to each of us:

> You are the light of the world. A city built on a hill cannot be hid. No one after lighting a lamp puts it under the bushel basket, but on the lampstand, and it gives light to all in the house. In the same way, let your light shine before others, so that they may see your good works and give glory to your Father in heaven.[3]

---

3. Ibid., Matthew 5:14–16.

Childhood

GRANDMA'S KITCHEN

Sunday evenings
around the table
in Grandma's kitchen
with only the women
made a lasting impression
on prepubescent male me.

Bubbly female warmth
suffused the atmosphere
along with the sweet
sugary smells of
baked cake and cookies
my two brothers and I
could hardly wait to eat.

One such evening
my favorite aunt
picked up my hand
from underneath
so as to see my fingernails,
saying "Look at those cuticles!
Full half-moons!
Why aren't mine like that?"

I felt the stirrings
of something I didn't understand—
a little flutter of the heart
about her holding my hand,
but I wasn't yet a man,
maybe eight or nine.

I was the oldest grandchild:
loved that position
and this attention.
I'd never heard of cuticles
nor noticed mine, but was
entranced by the feminine
energy I was swimming in.

I had no sisters,
just two younger brothers;
and my Dad's masculinity
predominated at home—
leaving my mother's energy
subdued at home, but amplified
in her mother's kitchen.

Being in that atmosphere—
surrounded with safety,
nurture, and fecundity—
awakened a nascent
sexuality in me,
aroused my own
latent masculinity.

A year or so later,
I found myself sitting in the
other room with the men.
I don't recall that transition.
Something was definitely lost,
something also gained.
Sexuality and gender
were somehow framed
by those two rooms.

But deep inside of me
Grandma's kitchen remained,
sustaining my sensitive side
and being also an inner sanctuary
to which I retreated,
and in which I hid
amidst the chronic fear
of punishment by my Dad,
who watched me and hit me
if I expressed myself
in a way he disapproved of.

ONE LEGACY OF TRAUMA

I was almost always
scared of my Dad
as a child and
even as a teen,
until I left home
for college at seventeen.

I was always on guard,
fearing he'd hit me
or give me an unhappy look
accompanied with what seemed
like barely contained intensity:
I was on constant alert.

I felt safest around him
in church, and usually when
visiting aunts, uncles, and cousins,
or grandparents on Sunday evenings;
somewhat safe when away from him
doing my chores or what pleased him.

But even then I felt haunted—
my inner scary Dad was
well-planted and daily watered
because we lived on a farm and
he was almost always around
unless in the field or in town.

During my early elementary
school years, I escaped
into reading. It was one way
I could leave the farm and him.
The world of reading soon became
in itself a beloved thing.

I was so absorbed one day
that I was late to do my chores,
which included feeding the cows
a special mix of supplements and grain
as they entered the barn to be milked
and were locked into their stanchions.

Suddenly, while lost in my reading,
I heard the house door open,
felt my Dad's furious energy, heard him
saying, "You get your ass out there
to do your chores; and next time I'm
coming after you with a pitchfork!"

That was probably the last time
I was caught with my guard down.
But the legacy of that event
has been a lifelong low-level
anxiety whenever I'm reading—
which distracts me to this day.

It doesn't take much to re-
constellate what I felt that day:
a mushy mix of self-betrayal,

gripping fear, flooding shame,
relief at being only threatened,
and a resolve saying, "Never again!"

Though now largely latent,
an inner sentinel's always on alert
for the lurking internal voice
that says I should be
doing something else before—
or instead of—enjoying reading.

The legacy of this trauma is that
what would otherwise have been
a valuable maturational lesson
in learning to balance work and pleasure,
instead pitted one against the other
in a way that handicaps me to this day.

TRANSFIGURATION AT GRANDMA'S FUNERAL

My maternal uncle Henry, whom everyone called Hank, had epilepsy; and in the 1950's in Iowa, drugs hadn't yet been developed nor made available which would have enabled him to live a fairly normal life. He lived with his parents/my grandparents, and when I was a child my parents and two brothers and I visited my grandparents at least twice a month. On some of those visits, I witnessed Uncle Hank having petit mal seizures—or "spells," as we called them—and at least twice grand mal seizures, all of which terrified me and made me feel so bad for Uncle Hank.

A major crisis in Uncle Hank's life, and in the life of the whole family, was when Grandma became sick. In addition to birthing ten children, she'd worked hard her whole life: raising all those children; cooking; cleaning; laundering; planting, tending and harvesting a garden; and living with Grandpa. She was a warm-hearted, generous, long-suffering wife, mother, and grandmother. At sixty years of age, she was diagnosed with lung cancer.

Everyone was devastated. I remember clearly to this day her and Grandpa driving onto our farmyard and coming into the house to tell my mother the diagnosis. She and my mother fell into each other's arms weeping inconsolably.

As the oldest daughter of eight younger siblings, my mother was something of a surrogate mother to those siblings and almost a sister to her mother. They had always talked to each other at least once a day every day on the phone, and I knew that from that moment forward my mother was wondering what she'd do when her mother was gone. I don't remember much else about that visit. I was twelve years old then.

Afterwards, I heard my parents talking about the fact that Grandma would be getting radiation treatments to shrink the tumor, and I don't know if they said—or I feared or surmised—that there'd be no cure and it would be a matter of time. I do recall my Mom saying to my Dad that Grandma had always said that she hoped Hank would die before she did. I'm not sure if it was implied, but I made the assumption that Grandma not only didn't want to leave Hank motherless, but also feared leaving him alone with Grandpa.

Grandma did live for several months, but then she died in hospital at the relatively young age of sixty-one, when I was thirteen. Hers was the first funeral I'd ever gone to, though I had gone several years before to a Wake for Grandpa's father (my maternal great-grandfather), which was held in Grandpa's brother's (my great-uncle's) home. I recall sitting on folding chairs in their large living room, looking somewhat curiously and uncomprehendingly at his body laid out in the open casket.

I didn't go to the Wake for Grandma, but did go to her funeral in her church. Her casket was open in the front of the sanctuary, and I sat with my parents and brothers in a pew in this church I'd never been in before. Which reminds me that after Grandpa left our church over never being elected an Elder, and before he joined the very small church where he was made Elder, he'd decided that he and Grandma would join this other church in the same town as ours. They were members there when Grandma died.

Her funeral that day was the occasion of my first transcendent, or spiritual, experience—though in hindsight, I'm sure that the way had been prepared for me by a story that I had overheard my mother telling my father: on the day of her death, Grandma's youngest daughter, my Aunt Joanne, was sitting with her in the hospital. By that time, my grandmother had been bedridden for weeks, was rarely conscious, and hadn't spoken for days. Suddenly—my Aunt Jo reported—Grandma raised her hand, got Jo's attention, and said, "Nearer my God to thee"; whereupon her hand dropped back down onto her bed and she died a few minutes thereafter.

I was transfixed by that story.

At the funeral service, there was an Order of Worship very similar to what I was accustomed to, but with the unusual addition of a male quartet scheduled to sing. I had noticed this in the Order of Worship—which we called the Bulletin—but I was unprepared for what happened inside me.

When it came time for them to sing, the men in the quartet stood up where they had been sitting in the choir loft behind the pulpit. They were backlit by light from the stained-glass window-portrait of Jesus behind them. In pure male harmony, they began to sing "Nearer my God to Thee," and I entered another world. It was the very hymn whose title my grandmother had uttered just before she died. I was transported. I perceived and experienced them as angels singing those words, not mere men. In some mysterious way, I was in a spiritual dimension united with God, my grandmother, and the angels; while at the same time sitting there in that church pew.

I was deeply, profoundly moved. The experience changed my life, made me aware of a spiritual dimension to the world that I'd heard about but had never experienced until now. I'd been baptized by water as an infant, but now I'd been baptized by the Spirit, I'd say. I felt nearer to God, and God felt nearer to me—like I was being held or upheld more securely in an other-worldly way while also clearly in the world as I knew it, and like I was part of a different family while still being in my own family.

I'd barely come back to earth by the time the Service ended. We all filed past the open casket, and I dared a last look at Grandma. I sobbed and stumbled as I walked past, but I'm sure I was helped to let her go and continue on my way in the assurance that she was with God and God was with me. I somehow knew that Grandma was all right, and so was I. That song and all it meant was an unforgettable, life-changing, life-sustaining experience.

I was so entranced by what was happening to me that I have no memory of Uncle Hank at that Service. I'm sure he was in shock, perhaps unable to take in the reality of his mother actually being dead. I don't know. I think that he rarely attended church services—for fear he'd have a seizure, be embarrassed, cause a scene, and disrupt the Service. I hope that he, too, felt upheld and sustained by that service to something of the same extent that I did.

Youth

MUSCLES

That early morning muscle stiffness
was a daily experience those summers
when I worked on a construction crew
with my Uncle Junior in my teens.

Long days of heavy physical labor
left me tired and hungry at end of day,
but I'd sleep well enough at night
that getting up at six wasn't too difficult.

Lunch bucket and thermos in hand,
we'd be at the jobsite around seven-thirty,
and the usually brisk morning air felt great
as my uncle spelled out what we'd do that day.

During the first hour or so of whatever
construction work I was engaged in,
there'd be this mysteriously warm enlivening
feeling inside, of tight muscles gradually loosening.

Whatever recovery from the previous day
was still going on, along with resistance
to another day's work, my muscles gradually
warmed up, literally and figuratively,

to working in fluid interactive harmony
with my will: a feeling similar to the one I've had
through the years and now fifty years later
when I do various deliberate stretches

upon awakening, after hiking, mowing the lawn,
or any form of labor, exercise, or even inactivity:
a blissful feeling that I'm an embodied me—
which I first became conscious of in my teens:

my body in motion in whatever space
I inhabit, executing some purposeful
act of will, while inside under my skin my
muscles move in their own space being me.

FIRE IN SULLY, IOWA, 1967

Those leaping flames in the dark of night
Shocked me awake, the red flashing light
Even two blocks away as if right outside.

Those side-by-side windows in that upstairs room
On the second floor of my parents' home
Faced east towards the center of my little hometown.

I leapt out of bed, my heart beating fast,
Dashed down the stairs to wake up my Dad;
I don't even remember exactly what I said.

We hurriedly dressed and ran towards the fire;
By the time we arrived the flames were even higher.
The fire truck came screaming around the corner.

A couple other men were already there,
Carrying out boxes from the burning store.
We tried to figure out what we were good for.

I'd never been so close to that kind of heat.
Everyone there was covered with sweat.
Suddenly water from the fire hose started to jet.

What happened next I couldn't have imagined:
The hose thrashing 'round like a giant python;
The power of the pump had ripped it free of the men.

On the end of that hose was a heavy metal coupling,
Which along with the hose was violently whipping.
Had it hit someone, it would have been crippling.

It took three men to finally grab the hose;
Meanwhile, of course, the fire was getting worse.
Both the fire and the water were extremely dangerous.

Finally the water was directed at the fire;
The "fire department" men were all volunteer;
Fought fires like this only a couple times a year.

Before very long, they'd put the fire out.
The flames gave way to billowing smoke;
The rafters still standing had a charcoal coat.

The entire experience was like a waking dream:
Surreal, extraordinary, happening at four a.m.
I felt like a boy though I was actually nineteen.

As my Dad and I slowly ambled back home,
New morning light was just beginning to dawn.
I still felt weird having entered their bedroom.

But nothing about that was ever said;
Crises like fire turn "normal" on its head.
We told Mom about it; couldn't go back to bed.

OASES IN THE DESERT OF DAD

The seventy-year-old male Presenter
at a Clinical Case Conference
showed videos of his therapy
with two small traumatized children
and one twenty-year-old Veteran
with PTSD from the Iraq War.

The Presenter's soothing voice
and confident, low-key manner
as he identified core wounds
and respectfully elicited
his patients' permission
and cooperation in touching—
sometimes literally—
their bound-up trauma
and drawing upon their
inner healing energy . . .
left me weeping
and profoundly re-inspired
about the healing work we do.

Surprisingly, then, the next day
I felt almost as sad
as I've ever been,
and for a couple of hours
I couldn't figure out why.

Then it came to me:
I was grieving the fact
that I hadn't had a Dad like that:
his soothing voice—
the intonation
carefully calibrated
to the patient's age
and injury;

his tender touch;
his sensitivity to
the patient's wound;
his profound respect
for the patient's need
to regulate the closeness;

his loving interest
in the innate
autonomous unfolding
of the patient's health-seeking drive
towards healing and growth;
his supporting, and when necessary
gently guiding that process,
rather than controlling
or punishing based on
his own agenda;

in sum: his finely honed
ability to effectively
express his loving support
was awesomely moving!

No wonder I was weeping
while observing
him in action; and then
feeling profoundly sad
when I realized more fully
what I had longed for and
gotten very little of
from my Dad.

Now of course,
the kind of father I wanted
doesn't exist.
This Presenter had honed
his art over forty years;
and I have certainly not
been the kind of father
that I wanted to be either.

I was afraid of my father
throughout my childhood.
I never felt safe with him
because of his angry outbursts
and because he'd hit me
without warning
as punishment until
my spirit was broken—
into compliance by age seven
and vigilance thereafter.

Years and years later—
as I discovered the dark
and scary depths
of my own psyche
while parenting my son—
did I realize that
my Dad was parenting me
the way he'd been parented;
and so as not to be crippled
by his disillusionment,
rage, and longing,
he'd entombed those
feelings in an almost airtight
edifice bolstered by a
judgmental, punitive God
who supposedly loved
but loved so conditionally that
there was hardly any hope
of feeling safe and loved.

When I—as a baby and
young child—expressed any
of these feelings, which
echoed his, he had to
smack them down and me also
to keep those same feelings
of his own from emerging.
They had to be locked down
and under his control,
as therefore did I.

Fortunately, when that same dynamic
occurred between me and my son,
I was in psychotherapy, and was
increasingly able to understand
that I was trying to keep
my own feelings under wraps
as much or more than my son's.

Oh, such anguish and regret, though,
about how I'd treated my son
and also myself: shutting down
those painful feelings,
along with now feeling
all those feelings
that I'd kept the lid on
over the years.

I still experience, suffer,
and wrestle with those feelings,
but I've also come to know
that the expression
of those feelings in a
loving relationship
is where healing lies,
where Divine Spirit is present,
and where I learn
to lovingly be with myself
in all aspects of my life,
including writing poetry.

This is the context
in which I remember
some tender moments
in the desert that was
life with my Dad.

At a men's softball game
on a summer evening
in our Iowa hometown,
when I was about thirteen,
I overheard my Dad
and another man
on the bleachers
talking about their kids:
I heard my Dad say
to that man, with
a certain amount of pride,
that "this one,"
nodding towards me,
"is gonna go to college."

That's how I learned of
his aspirations for me.
I felt a mixture of emotions:
A bit warmed that he was
even thinking of me
and of my future
separate from his;

some anxiety about whether I
could live up to those expectations;
affirmed that he recognized
my intelligence; and
embarrassed and awkward
at being the object
of positive attention.

His pronouncement about me
to another person did indeed
blaze a path for me
into the future, my future.

At around that same age,
I learned that I could hurt him.
We three sons would each
receive one gift at Christmas.
I rarely if ever asked
for what I wanted—which
was my way of protecting
myself from disappointment.

From an early age,
I had somehow learned
to hold together inside
both a desire for something
as well as an even stronger
insistence that I didn't
want that desired thing.

That year I risked letting
my Mom know that
I'd like a sweater;
other kids had them:
it would be my first sweater.

When it came time
for handing out the gifts,
the box was big enough
to contain a sweater.

I opened it, and to my dismay,
I immediately didn't like the color.
I must have blanched.
I myself hadn't fully realized
that I'd wanted a blue sweater.
I was so not used to asking
for anything that it had never
occurred to me to mention
to my mother the color I wanted.

I said, "Oh, it's tan," and
in a matter of milliseconds
I saw the pain in my Dad's face
when he heard my disappointment,
and my mother quickly said
"Your Dad picked it out;
isn't it a nice color?"

No one said anything further.
It was tan, camel-colored.
I don't remember ever wearing it,
don't know what happened to it.
I registered the experience
as evidence that if you ask
for something, you'll not get it;
and as for my Dad,
I can still see that pained look
on his face.

I see now in hindsight that
I was too young at that point
to fake gratitude, to
graciously receive his gift.
He'd tried to give me something;
but it was a color he liked.
He'd never bothered to ask,
nor had I dared to be specific
about what I wanted.
I don't remember Christmases
after that one.

Perhaps a year or so earlier,
when I was twelve
I'd noticed that my mustache
had become noticeable;
but of course I said nothing;
I just started sneakily using
my Dad's shaving cream and razor.

A couple of weeks later,
my mother told me that my Dad
had bought me my own razor.
Nothing was ever said
between him and me about it;
which led me to continue
to feel ashamed of my pubescence.

One occasion of unalloyed
pleasure in my Dad's company
happened when I was fourteen
as he was overhauling
the engine of one of the earliest
farm tractors ever made,
called the F-20. "Overhauling"
meant taking the engine
almost entirely apart,
cleaning the parts,
then reassembling it.

I was observing my Dad
do this, and as he lifted
the pistons out of their cylinders,
I said, "They aren't supposed to
be that black, are they, Dad?"
To which he replied, "No, sir,
they're black as Coalee's butt!"

I burst out laughing,
and he said "What?"
I managed to say,
"You said 'Coalee's butt.'"

"Oh that," he said, and now
he laughed a bit too; adding,
"that's an old expression
we had when I was a kid.
We had this huge black horse
on the farm who'd pull plows,
wagons, and other machinery,
which meant we were always
riding or walking behind this
horse we'd named Coalee.
His rear end was an everyday
part of our lives, so we'd say—
about anything really black—
"Black as Coalee's butt."

It was just my Dad and me
sharing an unguarded moment
unmediated by any other person,
and doing "man things"—maybe
the first time I felt almost
like a fellow "man" with him.

Two or three years later,
I had begun to use a real necktie,
not those weird clip-ons
we'd had to wear when younger.
A friend of mine had taught me
how to tie it. Then one Sunday,
my Dad carefully approached me

and showed me how to tweak
the knot a bit, comradely adding
that doing so made it look better.

It was a tender moment:
even though he was correcting me,
I experienced him as
fatherly, meaning to help me.

He made a similar intervention
once about a toy wooden barn
I'd built in our basement tool shop.
I had enjoyed building the barn:
I was refining my skills and
had taken it to the next level.
Then one day from the basement
he yelled upstairs to me, "Carroll,
come down here a minute."
My heart dropped to my toes:
I expected to be reprimanded
about something—no idea what—
but tremblingly went downstairs.

"I see you've made a barn," he said;
"it would be a little stronger here
if you added some reinforcement."
I was so relieved that I wasn't
going to be punished for something
that I said nothing, just nodded.
I began to breath normally again.

He had still said nothing positive,
but I knew he meant to be helpful.
This incident is representative
of how guarded and afraid
I was of him till I left home.

By then, of course,
I had internalized
his high expectations
and what I later realized were
exacting standards of excellence.
I assessed myself by those
same standards, and have
struggled to become
less demanding and less
judgmental of others
as well as myself.

Years later, I also noticed
and realized that my Dad
found it difficult to be
tender towards himself.
He could at times be that way
with my mother, and much
more so with his grandchildren:
with them, he could be more
the way he hadn't been with me.

My understanding of him—
not to mention

compassion and forgiveness—
were a long time coming.

A penultimate tender experience
with him happened about
five or six years before he died.[1]
I'd gone to visit him and my mother
with the usual ambivalence
about being with him.

At one point during that visit,
he asked me about my ministry
as a Pastoral Psychotherapist
in a way that was different
than how he had asked before.

He was asking open-ended questions
this time, instead of questions to which
I knew what answer he wanted,
which I'd experienced as hectoring,
and which I immediately resented,
and which I'd usually respond to
by withdrawing and hiding my real self
rather than engage in a wearisome
one-sided, supposedly open
promulgation of his evangelical
views of how I should do therapy—
from which I'd emerge browbeaten,
angry, wondering why I'd come.

---

1. Arkema, "Goodbye to Dad," 11–20.

Hark! This time, I don't know why,
he asked open-ended questions,
was genuinely interested in
what I had to say; he was even
pleasantly surprised, impressed,
and willing to learn!
Because of that,
I was then able to relax,
became fully present, and
I even surprised myself at
the clarity with which I
talked about my work!

My mother was attentive, too;
In fact, the change in him
may have been due to her
physical health increasingly
failing that year prior.
He was confronted with
death approaching her—
something new in his world
which he couldn't control.

I think it cracked his shell.
He had to let something
new into his world, and
he went with it more.
His strongest coping resource
was his Faith, but perhaps
Death's approach called into

question his airtight system,
and he was ready for new
insights, new understandings
of divine presence in life.

In any case, for the first time
with me, he listened, and
I think he understood that
God is present in process,
relationships, uncertainty,
helplessness, and fear.

The essential difference
between our stances was
in my having learned to
notice what the Spirit
is already always doing
instead of thinking one has
to bring or insert Holy Spirit
into the person or situation.

The former involves being a
witness to what the Spirit
is doing in a given context,
rather than coming across as
a condescending colonizer.

Hope appeared that day
for him and for me,
and for our relationship.

Young Adulthood:
My Vocational Choice

WILLIS P. DEBOER

"Could I see you after class
for a minute, Mr. Arkema?"
My heartbeat quickened;
I anticipated criticism.
What could this be about?

Good guy as I was—
a sophomore in college,
who said nothing in classes
unless called upon,
who wanted not to be seen—

why, in this my first
Religion Class
at Calvin College,
did Dr. DeBoer
want to see me?

Now it's true that this day—
in the seventh class
of the semester—

I had emerged from
my self-imposed silence

and had volunteered to
offer the Closing Prayer—
which DeBoer had invited
students to take turns doing
at the end of each class.

Though I'd been terrified that
I wouldn't be able to speak,
at a deeper level,
I trusted a part of me—
or was It God in me?

"Dear God, we're thankful
for this class and
for the opportunity
to learn more about You;
to feel Your presence

in silence as well as in speech.
Open our minds
and our hearts
to know You better
and to do Your will. Amen."

I'd surprised myself
at what I'd said,
relieved that
I could even speak
without faltering.

I gathered my folder
with notes from the lecture
and walked with
a queasy roiling feeling
to where he was standing.

"Mr. Arkema," he said,
"that was a remarkable prayer!
Why haven't you
been speaking up in class?
You must speak up more."

It took me a few seconds
to shift from certain
anticipated punishment
to hearing and feeling
that he was being positive.

I felt a bit chided, yes,
but more so, seen,
known, affirmed—
invited and challenged
to emerge from hiding.

This tiny experience
changed my life—
was an affirmation
of the risk I took
in volunteering to pray.

DeBoer was a key person
in my ongoing journey
of accepting my intelligence
and beginning to believe
that I had something to say.

He was a tall, erect
man with a strong voice
and a subtly playful
intelligence: he enjoyed
students, loved teaching.

Teaching for him was *educare*:
"leading forth" what's within.
He was just the person
I needed to help me do that.
I'll never forget him.

AFRAID TO PREACH

Having decided
while in college
to study for the ministry,
I applied to Princeton Seminary,
was accepted, and
I matriculated there.

Ministers, of course, preach,
but I was terrified
of public speaking;
I had had an almost
dissociative experience
while delivering

the mandatory speech
in high school Speech class,
and I hadn't felt
any differently
giving the required
speech in college.

My knowledge that
there were at least two
Preaching Classes in Seminary
which I'd be required to take
lay in the pit of my gut
like a gnawing dread.

I avoided taking those classes
as long as possible—
rationalizing that I would
opt to be an Associate Pastor
or find a Pastoral job that
didn't involve preaching.

But taking one of those
classes was inevitable.
I chose the soft-spoken
more mild-mannered
Professor whom I felt
least intimidated by.

It never occurred to me
to talk to him or
anyone else about my fears.
But it didn't take long
for his experienced eye
to see that I was in trouble.

He had laid a solid
physiological foundation
for how to use one's diaphragm
to relax, breathe deeply,
and project one's voice
while speaking in public.

This was new and helpful
information for me;
but even so, after I'd read

in a mortified monotone
some poetry and scripture
he'd given us to read in class,

he pulled me aside one day
to say that there was
a Faculty Associate
whom he thought
could be helpful to me—
a retired female actress

named Virginia Damon;
that I should contact her
for a Speech lesson. I did.
We met—just the two of us—
in this immense
corner room upstairs

in ancient ugly Stuart Hall.
The thick stone walls
were like pillars between
many elongated windows
which soared upward
towards the sky-high ceiling.

Ms. Damon—standing on the floor
between the desk on its dais
and the door—suggested that
I go across the enormous room,
stand looking out the window,
and just tell a story, any story.

This radically unconventional
arrangement in this staid
but spacious old room in a
revered theological seminary
shocked me out of my superego
to think maybe I could think for myself.

I felt for the first time free
of the daunting responsibility
of preaching God's Word.
She was inviting me
to tell my own story—
any story I chose!

I momentarily drew a blank,
but as I stood looking out
the window, I saw a squirrel,
and I began to tell about
how I used to hunt squirrels—
shoot and kill them for sport.

Having grown up on a farm in Iowa,
my Dad had given me permission—
when I turned sixteen—
to buy my own single-shot rifle.
In that place and time,
this was not uncommon.

I loved hunting,
and became a good shot.
I'd walk a quarter-mile

alone to the back pasture—
free of Dad for a few hours,
and from farm work and chores.

It was peaceful being amongst
the ancient oak and maple trees,
patiently waiting for a squirrel
to poke its head out of a hole
in a tree, then take aim and shoot.
More often than not, I'd hit it.

But something deep inside
began to bother me: why
am I doing this? Rationalizing
that squirrels were plentiful, I
continued hunting for a few more months,
but soon accepted that I'd lost the heart for it.

I had loved the challenge
of hitting the target; but
trying to outwit a squirrel—what
kind of cheap rigged odds was that?
I didn't need nor eat the meat,
so I gave it up. I quit hunting.

I'd become increasingly clear
that what I loved most
was the peace and quiet—
being by myself in nature,
free of my brothers, the watchful
eye of my Dad, and work.

When I finished telling this story,
I felt somehow redeemed—
both because I'd stopped hunting
but more because I'd found something
new in myself: an inner grounding
in this personal experience

of the Spirit's patient presence
incarnate in Virginia Damon:
congratulatory, warmly affirming,
conveying that she knew I could do it.
This was a one-time experience,
the mere beginnings of confidence,

but a pivotal step in my journey
of tuning the instrument of my body
and beginning to believe—have hope—
that I might become more adequate
to the task of public speaking
and a bit less afraid of preaching.

Formation as a Pastor

ONE THING SHE SAID, ONE THING SHE DID

As a compliant good guy—
who of course then
had fathoms
of denied
and repressed anger—
I wanted to be a minister.

I graduated from Princeton Seminary,
did well there academically,
as I had also
in college;
but that was head-knowledge . . .
Afraid of congregational ministry,

I enrolled for nine months
in a Chaplain Residency
Training
Program
in a General Medical
Hospital in West Philadelphia.

I was supervised by Joan—a female
Chaplain—both individually and
in a group

once a week
to learn from my patient visits
how to become a Healing Presence.

The structure of the program
fostered personal as well as
professional
self-discovery—
which meant discerning one's
strengths as well as limitations.

At one point during those nine months
Joan said something which
changed
my life:
I'd been talking in the group
about a patient and her family,

and Joan, listening, smiled and said,
"Did you hear yourself use the word
"fascinating"
as you were
talking about the family's dynamics?"
I actually had not been aware of this,

but her energy brought me up short;
whereupon I realized that
I had been
talking
with a kind of intensity
that revealed my fascination.

* * *

I had come to know and trust Joan
and her observations about me.
What she would
say rang true,
and came from a stance
of listening and hearing me, then

highlighting what came from inside out
of me, rather than prioritizing how well
I complied
with her
or the Program's criteria
or expectations of a Student Chaplain.

Her comment about my fascination
helped me notice, know, and
define
myself,
and to begin to trust and build
an identity around what fascinated me!

* * *

With regard to my repressed anger,
it began to emerge in the context
of my trusting
relationship
with Joan—as such feelings do
once it becomes safe to express them.

My anger initially came out
in a passive-aggressive way:
I stopped
preparing
for individual supervision in
the required way I had agreed to.

I was half-consciously arriving
at our supervisory sessions
without
verbatims—
written accounts of my talks
with patients whom I had visited.

I see now in hindsight that
I was testing how Joan
would
respond
if I was not the compliant
good guy I had begun to tire of.

Joan asked me why I was no longer
bringing in verbatims.
I actually
didn't know.
I was still mostly unconscious of
my anger about complying with Authorities.

She said she really didn't want to
take this stance, but that
until

I came
prepared with a verbatim,
she was suspending supervision.

I felt relief, shame, abandoned by her,
even though I had broken our
contractual
relationship.
I also felt disoriented;
but talked about it with a peer,

who loved me into understanding
the opportunity that lay in this:
a new me
emerging!
She thus reframed it as growth
and encouraged me to talk with Joan.

I contacted Joan and returned to
supervision, verbatim in hand,
uneasy,
but hopeful.
Joan agreed that something new
was emerging, and we laughed.

This nonjudgmental reframing of my anger
by both Joan and my colleague—
both of them
female—
helped me begin to integrate my
anger and its energy into my self

as an enlivening and potentially
empowering feeling which
I needn't be
afraid of,
but could begin to put into words—
like telling Joan I hated doing verbatims!

Again, we laughed. Joan understood
how vulnerable I felt exposing
my pastoral
conversations
with patients, and I'd come to
trust her because she modeled

that she could be ambivalent
about being firm, but be
assertive
and firm
nonetheless, thus helping me
modify my judgmental superego.

*   *   *

Thus in that relationship with Joan
I began to define myself
and become
more whole.
I learned to notice what fascinates me,
and that anger can be constructive energy.

Of course this was just a beginning:
I was only twenty-four.
It has taken—
and is continuing
to take—all the years since then
to refine and actualize what I learned.

I subsequently entered Parish Ministry,
which had a broad range
of pastoral
responsibilities;
but in the first year or two
I noticed how much I loved counseling.

Trusting what I'd learned with Joan—
to pay attention to what
I loved—
I enrolled
in a psychotherapy training program,
and have been a Therapist ever since.

SUPERVISING THE ANGRY STUDENT/SUPERVISEE

I'll use myself as the subject of this Case Study about dealing with an Angry Student/Supervisee in Psychotherapy Training. I'll present a chronological sequence of incidents, over several years, which were incrementally pivotal in helping me deal with my anger—which is of course a continuing journey.

For some family-of-origin and characterological background to these incidents, I'll mention that I was an angry, rather self-righteous twenty-six-year-old Clinical Pastoral Education [CPE] student who didn't even know how angry I was. I'm a white male born and raised on a small farm in central Iowa; the oldest of three brothers; and my nuclear and extended families—both maternal and paternal—are Dutch, and members of the Christian Reformed Church. My parents were second-generation immigrants. I had a nice-guy, quiet, compliant persona—or "false/adaptive self," in Winnicott's language—[1]which kept my anger repressed by a powerful superego and which masked my fear, sadness, and shame. As a child, I lived in chronic fear of my father's occasional spankings/beatings if my behavior met with his disapproval. My father held me—as the oldest of three sons—responsible for any problems that arose between my brothers and me; so I learned at about age six to distance myself from my brothers and thus have minimal interaction with them. I also used what intelligence I had to vigilantly detect what might displease my father; I not only avoided displeasing him but also literally worked exceptionally hard on the farm in an effort to please him.

In Elementary School, my smiling, self-protective mask at times just cracked when called upon or corrected; I would be unable to keep smiling, and the underlying sadness, fear, and shame would break through. I'd feel mortifyingly exposed. In High School, I put my head into books and studying, avoiding many interactions that way, including dating. This focus and way of coping continued through college. I did get excellent grades, and I did

---

1. Winnicott, "Ego Distortion," 140–152.

have one good male friend from second grade through college, but had only a few dates with girls in college.

The Fall after graduation from college, I went to Princeton Theological Seminary [PTS] in 1970, met a woman there, and married her the next April. I continued to study a lot, and did well academically, but my emotions were so repressed that I was usually ill at ease with myself when with other people. My persona, however, enabled me to get along quite well, even in my Field Education on Sundays in a parish.

During summers while in Seminary, I worked as a Counselor at a residential Drug Rehabilitation Center in which a "professional" counselor like myself was paired with a recovering addict to lead therapy groups and—of all things—anger workshops. Almost all of the residents were recovering from heroin addiction, and they were enrolled—sometimes by Court mandate—at the Center for one to two years.

The structure of the Anger Workshops was that one Resident would confront another Resident with whom he/she was angry. They would sit on chairs facing each other, in a "fishbowl" setting in which the entire community—Staff and Residents—sat in a huge circle surrounding them. The angry Resident would express her/his anger in a loud voice, often yelling until her/his anger was spent; and then the other could respond in the same way. I was transfixed by these encounters.

In hindsight, I realized that my immersion in this Program was transformative for me: and was the beginning of the de-repression of my own anger, though it took several years before I dared openly express my anger in a relational way.

In addition to the Anger Workshops, there were Therapy Groups, in which the Residents were supported in the telling of their stories of their childhood and adolescent traumas with which they had coped by using drugs. The intensity and vulnerability of these Residents telling their histories in these groups was shocking, awesome, expansive and deepening of my world—giving me a first-hand witnessing of, and participation in, healing possibilities. This was my first exposure to Psychotherapy, and to the fact that anger could be openly expressed in a mostly constructive way. I'm still grateful to the Spirit for leading me to that Program for two summers; and I still have vivid memories of the Group Leaders I was partnered with, and of some of the Residents in the Program. I eventually did twice-weekly Individual Therapy with a few Residents, and during my second year in Seminary, I worked there one day a week throughout the academic year.

In the Summer after my graduation from PTS (1974), I took a Basic Quarter of Clinical Pastoral Education [CPE] at a State Mental hospital, in which I was a Student Chaplain assigned to two Wards of patients as my "parish." There were five other men in the Group, and we met once-weekly individually and once-weekly as a Group with the CPE Supervisor, KL, who was a veteran chaplain in his mid-sixties.

This group was called Open Group, a time for voluntary sharing and processing of our experiences and feelings as Student Chaplains at the hospital. By the third or fourth Group meeting, I had become very annoyed with one of my colleagues, D., who spent each session doodling (I sat next to him, and could see that he was doodling, and not even taking notes, which would have also been questionable to me) in a notebook and not participating in the discussions. At one point, I burst out, "D., what in the world are you doing?" He was startled, raised his eyes and said "What do you mean?" I said, "You sit there doodling in every Group and saying nothing!"

I don't recall clearly what happened after that. I'm sure that the Supervisor intervened in a facilitative way, and I myself was aware of having scared myself almost as much as D. by my anger. At the end of the Group session, as I was leaving, walking past the Supervisor, he reached out to shake my hand, saying, "Put 'er there, Tiger!" in an affirming congratulatory way. He had done some "damage control" with D. before the Group ended, because D. had said he thought he just wouldn't come back. [He did, but we were a bit awkward with each other for the remainder of the summer.]

I saw in hindsight that my anger had popped out in what I experienced as a safe place. To be sure, my anger was partly self-righteous superego anger. I was several years away from being able to handle my ego annoyance and anger in a relational way: being able to more calmly express my discomfort at D.'s withdrawal and my desire for him to participate. Nor did I realize till much later that I was projectively identifying with D., because he was behaving in a way similar to how I had behaved in most contexts (though I'd have been note-taking instead—such a "good guy" was I).

But the Supervisor's congratulations felt very affirming and empowering. Up until then, I couldn't have imagined receiving a positive, encouraging response to my anger. It was an important first step in integrating into my ego an energy that had been judged unacceptable and repressed by my superego.

One year after that Basic Quarter of CPE, I took three quarters of CPE (during the 1975-1976 academic year) at a General Medical Center. During those nine months, that persona that I mentioned earlier, began to further crack. I was in weekly supervision with a female Supervisor-in-Training, JH. The structure was that I'd present a verbatim record of some incident of being a Chaplain; we'd discuss the interaction, and I could learn how to be more effective in ministry. As you know or can imagine, it was impossible to present a "flawless" verbatim: there is no such a thing! I couldn't present an incident in which I was beyond critique and needed no improvement.

My ego was terrified, and still not well-equipped to hear critique as constructive and supportive of an expanding ego and developing professional skills. After three or four sessions, the Senior Chaplain/Supervisor, DA, sat in on our session in order to observe and experience the Supervisor-in-Training, JH, as a part of her process of maturing as a Chaplain Supervisor. I had previously given unthinking assent to his presence, and had already begun to get to know him, since he was a co-leader with JH of the weekly Open Group sessions (comprised of me and four other Chaplain Residents).

During that session when he was sitting in, I completely ignored him. After a few minutes, JH became uncomfortable, and asked me if I had any feelings about DA being there. I said no, but then when she noted that I was ignoring DA and hadn't even greeted nor acknowledged him, I looked at him, he met my eyes, and I said, "Well, yes, I guess I don't like it." She chuckled and said she wasn't fully comfortable with it either, but that she could learn from his observations of her, and asked me if I was okay with continuing? I said 'Yes," and I did feel better about it after our having addressed it.

Through that experience, I gradually became aware of my passive aggression, which I acted out even more clearly a few weeks later. I came to a supervisory session with JH with no verbatim and some lame excuse, which surprised her, but she went with it and suggested I just tell her about an incident which we could then discuss. We did that, and the next week again I brought no verbatim. At that point, she suggested we talk about why I wasn't doing what I had agreed to do. I didn't have any ideas about what was leading me to do this, nor was I particularly open to exploring motivations; so she said she hated to do this, but that she needed to suspend our sessions until I was willing to bring verbatims.

I was unable to identify or express it at that time, but I was feeling such shame over not being a "good boy" that I couldn't explore any other motivations. I resumed sessions the next week with a verbatim. A session or two later, she wondered if I had been passively expressing my anger at her for inviting DA to sit in during that previous session? I allowed that that was possible, and even later still—as we discussed it further—I became aware of my passive dependency: that I was wanting to regress to infancy; receive special favors from her; and not grow up and be an adult. All desires of which I was ashamed.

Meanwhile, the Open Group sessions continued, led by DA and JH, and I felt increasingly more at ease with expressing myself in the Group. In one of these meetings, we were talking about preaching (we took turns leading worship and preaching in the hospital Chapel on Sundays). On the Sunday just prior, I had attended a worship service elsewhere, in a Church, and a well-known sixty-something Preacher had strongly criticized the clothing and hair styles of young people those days. I was appalled at how superficial and hackneyed these comments were, and I felt deeply troubled that he was alienating future Church members! While recounting this in the Group, I banged my fist on the round table around which we were assembled for Group. I noticed one colleague jump a bit, and I had somewhat startled myself with this outburst, asking if I had hit the table quite hard? A male colleague said "Yes, very hard," whereupon DA said to JH, "That seems like an example of righteous indignation!"

I had been drifting into shame, but his comment and her laughing agreement relieved the tension and helped me lay claim to my anger and, without shame, begin to think constructively about the modulation of such feelings in an unashamed way.

Three years later, in 1979, while I was an Associate Pastor in parish ministry, I applied for admission to the Pastoral Psychotherapy Residency Training Program at the Blanton-Peale Graduate Institute [BP] in Manhattan. The final step in the application process was an Admissions Interview with three Faculty members. Prior to that interview, I had completed and submitted a great deal of paperwork and had written extensive responses to narrative questions in the Application.

The structure of the Interview Process was that one of the three faculty members was assigned to read the already submitted Application materials before the interview and "present" the Applicant to the Committee. In my interview, this Presenter took charge and asked me to introduce myself and talk about why I wanted to enter training. I began to do so, and then, for some uncanny reason, I asked the Presenter if he'd read my materials. I've always been intuitive, and I guess it was at work here. He said, "Well, actually, I have not"—a model of honesty, assertiveness, and humanity. I was taken aback, but in a surprising expression of my own courage, I managed to say, "Well, I guess I have feelings about that." He replied, "Well, so do I." We all laughed, and then he said, "I am sorry that I haven't read the materials. I know that writing it was a lot of work. Can you summarize it for us?"

The honesty and laughter mitigated my anger in the moment, and I was able to move on. I realize now too that his frank honesty helped me restore what I know in hindsight was a shaken trust in him and the Institute. I ended up with a sense that this was a place where Residents and Faculty could be authentic. The interview proceeded, went well, and I was accepted into the Program.

The next step in how my anger was dealt with happened two or three months into my first year of training at BP. I met weekly with a Pastoral Psychotherapist, DN, a Faculty member, for supervision of my caseload. One day, he was at least ten minutes late, which was unusual for him. I was anxious but pissed too—probably anxious because I was angry and unsure what to do about it. Partly out of being "good," pleasing authority figures, knowing what I "should" do, and partly because I was indeed annoyed, I said "I'm feeling angry that you're late." He stiffened just slightly and said "What are you going to do about it?" I was a bit taken aback, stumbled verbally, said something like "Well, I guess I'm telling you about it." He nor I processed it further, and he waited till I proceeded to present a case for supervision, as usual.

He had a quiet, minimally interactive, classical style of supervision, paralleling and/or modeling the more classical non-directive model of psychoanalytic psychotherapy. I found his response more unhelpful than helpful. It left my anger at him unresolved, and didn't repair the relationship/alliance; and I took away from that interaction that supervision with him was not a place to process my anger. It was "helpful" insofar it made clear that supervision is not therapy; that a certain deference to authority is important; and that the task at hand was presenting my work for supervision.

The classical model of psychoanalytic psychotherapy provides a basic foundation and structure upon which all therapy which leads to deep change is built, because when adhered to consistently and handled well-enough by the therapist, almost all aspects of it provide access to unconscious, archaic relationships, wounds, motivations, defenses/coping mechanisms, and characterological psychic structure. Uncovering all these, over time, can strengthen the ego—such that "where id was, there shall ego be,"[2] thus giving the ego more freedom to choose how to handle id and superego.

Belief in the repetition compulsion; exploration of resistance before content; exploring variations from the frame; recognizing transference and countertransference; and then allowing enough time for working through—that is, time for the patient to implement and integrate new behaviors and insights into her/his life and relationships—are all invaluable aspects of a good-enough analysis.

However, in the course of my own three personal analyses, plus group, marital, and family therapies, in addition to other supervisory experiences—as well as being a supervisor myself and in my own Practice as a Therapist, I have come to believe that this approach alone has serious limitations. As in the supervision just summarized, his approach didn't repair the alliance, didn't welcome my anger nor validate it, nor was my ego strengthened to deal with my superego or id.[3]

The object relations school; Kohutian self-psychology; intersubjectivity; attachment theories; and neuroscientific studies have all in unique ways, opened up the pre-oedipal (birth to age five) years of life to more nuanced understanding of the early psyche and more interactive ways of treatment—with more focus on strengthening the ego through a more interactive alliance between patient and therapist—though of course the needs and developmental level of the patient is primary, not the needs of the therapist.

These pre-oedipal approaches place more emphasis on mirroring, validations, nonverbal communication, early trauma—all still with a view towards ultimate verbalization and sublimation—sublime, creative expression—of one's feelings and impulses. In these approaches, there is a more nuanced interactive field between therapist and patient, such that there is an emotionally corrective experience in addition to cognitive insight, which together lead to deep change.

2. Freud, *The Ego*.
3. Celani, *Fairbairn's Structural Model,"* 50–83.

A centrally important factor in my coming to terms with my anger and in processing how it was dealt with by these various supervisors and teachers was my own personal therapy. After that first summer of Basic CPE in 1974 with KL as supervisor, I had gotten into Individual Therapy with a Pastoral Psychotherapist, JS, at KL's recommendation. KL made the suggestion in an ego-supportive rather than a pathologizing way. This first therapist JS was a gentle, mild, relaxed, and very intelligent man who normalized where I was developmentally—both emotionally and psychologically—and validated my feelings. I saw him weekly for 18 months until I moved from Philadelphia to the Newark, New Jersey, Associate Pastorate position in 1976. After I had terminated with JS, I invited him to give my Ordination Sermon, and he did. It was a sermon based on the text of Jesus healing the Gerasene demoniac (Mark 5:1–20), which focused on the fact that most people who witnessed the healing were more concerned about the economic loss of the pigs going off the cliff than on the remarkable healing. I remember weeping, feeling deeply understood and feeling affirmed in my Call to the Ministry of Healing, no matter how it would be viewed by others.

In 1977, my [now ex-] wife and I were in Marital Therapy for several months with another male Pastoral Psychotherapist, who was also licensed as a Marriage and Family Therapist. Then when I began the Residency Program at BP in 1979, I began twice-weekly Individual Psychotherapy with a female therapist, NF. Blanton-Peale required this of all Residents, as well as at least one year of Group or Couples therapy. I spent 18 months in Group therapy with NF while I was also seeing her Individually. She too was very supportive of my ego—listening to a great deal of pain and anger from my childhood. I had her in a positive mother-transference. In the Group Therapy, I continued to practice my assertiveness and shared some of my vulnerability as well as sexual feelings towards one woman in the group. I also received support and understanding of my marital frustrations and disappointments.

These therapies helped prepare me for the next crucial experience in dealing with my anger. In 1983, I was being supervised in my final year of Training at BP by the Senior Psychiatrist on the Faculty, WS. He was a brilliant, articulate, physically large man whom I was initially intimidated by, and onto whom it was easy for me to project my superego-negative father-transference. I was terrified of him at first, but had received enough validation, affirmation, and experience of my own abilities that I could talk with him about my fears of him in the first session. He listened, was curious about where these feelings were coming from, and was non-critical. He respected my abilities; highlighted the positive ways I was dealing with my clients; and presented alternative responses to clients in ways that made sense to me. I recall his excitement when I played a recording of a session in which I asked a female client a question about her sexual feelings.

Then one day something happened between him and me which changed my life. He was a few minutes late to our supervisory session. When he did come in, he asked me to wait a second while he checked his answering machine. I was incredulous, felt shocked, furious inside, but also very anxious; but when he finished checking his messages, I managed to say "I'm feeling angry about your being late and then checking your messages during my supervision." I could feel that he heard me and took me seriously; and he simply said, "Yes, anyone would be angry about that."

Such a brief and seemingly simple reply, but it changed my life! I felt tremendous relief, felt heard, understood, and validated in a way I never had before; and this from a man with whom I was working through a major negative father-transference.

This stands out for me as an exemplary model of how to deal with an angry student/supervisee. It wasn't therapy, and because I was and had been in several years of therapy (four years into my seven-year therapeutic relationship with NF), I didn't need to explore this further with him. It wasn't therapy, but it certainly was therapeutic. I found this interaction very healing; it strengthened my ego, mitigated my superego, and affirmed my self-assertiveness.

Our relationship was the container for two further self-assertions on my part towards him. On occasion, we switched our regular weekly supervisory location from an office at BP to his private office a few blocks away. On one of these occasions, I understood that we were meeting in his office; but he understood that we were meeting at BP. I went to the waiting room at his office, and he didn't show up till our session was almost over, whereupon he was surprised to see me. He insisted he'd made it clear that we were meeting at BP. I insisted on my understanding. I stood my ground, and we were able to get on with supervision the next week. I think I paid him anyway, which annoyed me, but I wasn't ready to withhold payment.

A few weeks later, he was an hour late for one of my two-hour Evaluations during my last year of Training, claiming he'd gotten tied up in traffic. The next time I saw him in supervision, I told him that I wasn't going to pay him for that missed hour. I could sense that he was a little surprised, and didn't like it, but he said, "Do what you want to do."

The final incident I want to cite, happened when I was a Teaching Fellow [1983-84] on the Faculty of BP, the year directly following my graduation. This incident falls in the territory of Supervisors "getting their own act together" about how they deal with their own and their students' anger.

I was now a Faculty Member, but also still a "student," in that I was in Supervision of Supervision with a Senior Member (JM) of the Faculty, because I was supervising Residents and Chairing some Residents' Evaluation Committees but I didn't yet have the necessary credentials to supervise independently.

Midway through that academic year as a Teaching Fellow, I was chairing a Resident's Evaluation Committee. In those evaluations, a Resident would read a previously written self-evaluation, and each of the Resident's supervisors (ranging from a minimum of two to five) would read her/his Evaluation of the Resident's progress, strengths, and weaknesses; then there would be discussion and recommendations, all facilitated by the Chairperson. During this Evaluation, the Resident was telling about her anger at someone (not someone in the room, and I don't think it was towards a patient of hers, but I don't remember whom), and I said something like "So you can get really angry!" There was a brief silence, during which I had a sense that I had stepped in something smelly. I had always experienced her as quiet, soft-spoken, demure; but even so, there was no excuse for what I said.

One of her supervisors—who was also my Supervisor of Supervision—said, with a certain amount of indignation himself, that it's important to not have a tone of judgment about a Resident's anger. I immediately felt chastened—agreeing inwardly with him, and ashamed of what I had done. I kept my outward composure enough to proceed with the Evaluation.

The Supervisor and I discussed it in my session with him later that week. Even before meeting with him, I was humbled at having been so judgmental of the Resident's strong anger, and in this case, I regretted the impact of my comment on the Resident and on the process of the Evaluation. I had been thrown off balance to such a degree in the aftermath of what I'd said, that as Chair I wasn't able to return to the Resident's anger in a way which could have been productive.

Through the many years since that incident, I have continued to deal with my anger and its various roots and permutations. What has helped me most to arrive at a better relationship with my anger has been to become aware of the pain and helplessness underneath it. The caring, curious, understanding, and compassionate presence of those therapists—and a few supervisors—with whom I've discussed and expressed my anger and its sources have normalized my anger and made it understandable to me, thereby strengthening my ego, giving me some distance from the feeling, and helping me to express it—more of the time—in constructive ways which maintain and even strengthen the relationship with the person I'm angry with in my current life.

I try not to defensively react when anger is coming at me from outside, nor let myself be taken over by it when it's coming from within me. This gives me enough distance from it to remain centered in my mature ego and then make informed and intelligent choices.

It's important to mention another thing which helped me to achieve a healthier relationship with my anger, which was that within months of moving East to attend PTS, I left the Christian Reformed Church [CRC]—during my first year at PTS (1974)—and joined the Presbyterian Church USA [PCUSA], in which I'm still an ordained clergyman serving in a validated ministry as a Pastoral Psychotherapist. I needed to leave the judgmentalism, exclusivism, and prescriptive and proscriptive orientation of the CRC, which I experienced as a climate of fear and guilt while giving lip-service to grace and love. I have felt more room to breathe and be creative in the PCUSA.

In summary, there are indeed some important techniques in dealing with a student/supervisee's anger, such as setting clear, consistent expectations and limits—actually a written "contract" can be best—and enforcing those (as JH did with me). But even when a contract is in place, how the Supervisor/Teacher maintains or enforces it will be influenced by his/her relationship with her/his own anger, as was the case with DN and JM, my Supervisor of Supervision.

Hopefully, the Supervisor/Teacher can accept his/her own and others' anger as a valid feeling arising from an understandable past or present experience; will not try to get into a power struggle (like DN with me) nor pathologize it nor shut it down (as I did with the Resident in her Evaluation); and will affirm the supervisee/student's constructive expression of anger (as did KL, DA, WS). A playful sense of humor helps also, as in my Admission Interview at BP.

Asking an exploratory, open-ended question—rather than a defensive/challenging question (as DN did)—can be a way of responding to the supervisee/student's expression of anger and moving through it to the task at hand (teaching/supervising).

It's also very important for the Supervisor/Teacher to accurately assess the supervisee/student's level of ego/psychological/emotional development in determining how to respond (as KL, JH, and WS did).

Finally, with regard to how a Supervisor/Teacher can best deal with a supervisee/student's anger, it's my opinion and experience that more important than any technique—or any other "how,"—is the Supervisor/Teacher's relationship with her/his own anger; because that will most likely be the primary factor in how he/she deals with a supervisee/student's anger. The Supervisor's own ongoing personal analysis and supervision are invaluable— at a minimum, ongoing self-analysis, and/or peer supervision/consultation.

Anger is a powerful energy, which can be harmful and destructive, but if managed and channeled by an integrated ego and superego, it can be remarkably motivating, creative, and productive. The more I de-repressed and learned how to better assert and express my anger, the more alive I became. At the same time, I felt more deeply relaxed and at peace inside. Anger is a powerhouse of energy, and greater access to it has helped me be more creative, playful, and productive, as well as continuing to help me set healthy limits and take better care of myself in personal and professional relationships.

Pastoral Psychotherapy

WORDS CREATE SELF AND WORLD

I've practiced the "talking cure"
for forty years and
have been healed by it myself,
but have only recently
gotten clearer about
why and how it works:

Words create the world.
"In the beginning was the Word."[1]
Vocalizations, cries, grunts,
babbling noises, syllables, words, all
constellate and communicate.

A baby's noises
express an inner state
to baby's own self
and to the world
outside inchoate

until parental presence
responds by capturing
the vocalization

---

1. The Holy Bible, John 1:1a.

into a word which
charms baby when heard.

Talk "cures" because
words create a coherent
world out of chaos
inside when it's heard
and reflected from outside.

The very existence
of vocalizations
is a manifestation
that we are in relationships—
social and individual agents

of an interaction
which creates a self—
separate yet
doomed to die
without being in-relation.

Words create invisible
inner psychic buildings
in which we live;
they also function
as external bridges
between self and other.

I once treated a couple
who sought help because
the husband was behaving

strangely, which scared the wife,
who feared he had dementia.

He'd previously been very active
in church and around the home.
Now he would disappear
on long walks or by car,
talk in non-sequiturs, he'd
dropped out of church activities.

I met with each of them
individually to obtain
a background history
of their entire lives
from childhood on.

I spent four sessions
guiding and listening
with detailed interest
to the husband tell his
fascinating life-story.

When we arrived back
at the present time,
he was a different man.
He'd come to know himself
in a coherent way

from me just listening
in a nonjudgmental way
to him review his life

with all its decisions
and twists and turns.

He'd stitched himself
back together again—
actually in a new way,
separately from whomever
his wife, his church, or

anyone else wanted him to be.
He'd come to appreciate
himself: he often laughed
or smiled at certain
occurrences and decisions.

We met once more
as a threesome;
his wife was relieved,
surprised, and pleased.
He was good to go.

Another client of mine
began wrestling with
the demon of drink
after his wife threatened
to leave him if he didn't.

He came to realize—
through our nonjudgmental
curiosity about his history—

that his college-age drinking
had helped free him

from strict parental
and religious prohibitions—
such that he had come alive,
explored new territory,
and was able to truly play!

Once we'd discovered
the positive function
of his drinking, he
was freed from thinking
of it only as a problem;

but it was now becoming
too much of a problem—
threatening the loss of his wife
as well as their two children.
Through our work, he came to realize

that he didn't need alcohol
any more to be who he is:
as an adult of forty years,
he didn't need alcohol
to be and play as he chose.

Near the end of our work
together, while reviewing
the process of change and growth,

he summarized the journey
with the phrase "memorializing."

I was awe-struck at the
creative application of that word—
which I'd usually associated
with cemeteries and death—
to the re-membering

and appreciation of a
lived and ongoing life:
an ability to step back,
observe, appreciate,
and reshape one's own life!

To "memorialize"—that is,
to commemorate the process
he'd undergone in talk therapy
to create a new life and identity
built on love of self and others.

Words organize, make sense, create
and re-create a self and a world.
Words create! The writer
of the gospel of John dares
to say that at the beginning

of everything is the Word,
and he even more arrestingly
says that the Word is

with God, and—get this—
that the Word IS God!

God as Creator, who has created
human beings in God's image,
has given humans the ability to create.
Human creativity can then be
understood as God in us!

The Hebrew scriptures
also begin with creativity
through God's word,
which says "Let there be . . . ,"
and each time "it was so."[2]

The original divine impulse—
or self-expression—is
to create, in expansive
yet intricate detail,
an interdependent world

in which even life and death
are part of the complex,
ever-renewing process
of a living organism dying
and feeding new life.

The Scriptures later
make it clear
that words can

---

2. Ibid., Genesis 1:1–2:3.

also angrily destroy—
even God's words.

The prophet Hosea
reveals the heart of God
being transformed from
destructive anger to
tender compassion:

"How can I give you up, Ephraim?
How can I hand you over, O Israel?
. . . My heart recoils within me;
my compassion grows warm
and tender. I will not execute

my fierce anger. I will not
again destroy Ephraim;
for I am God and no mortal,
the Holy One in your midst,
and I will not come in wrath."[3]

The original divine impulse
is to construct, to create
a harmonious whole,
and then when things go awry,
to redeem, to heal—

even to transform
God's own inner anger
and destructive impulses

3. Ibid., Hosea 11:8–9.

into suffering compassion
and self-sacrificial love.

God bears, endures,
moves through God's
own suffering
without trying
not to feel it and

without trying to
take control of it
by making others suffer—
which does for sure
let the other know

how the torturer feels;
but in the end
expands and justifies
an ever-escalating cycle
of non-redemptive violence.

When the apostle Peter
resorts to violence
to avoid suffering,
Jesus says,
"No more of this,"[4]

and heals the ear
of the arresting officer
that Peter had cut off.

4. Ibid., Luke 22:51.

Again, words heal
and create the world

that God wants us
to live in: to not
resort to violence,
but to work towards
creating a world

in which people
respect each other,
do justice, love kindness,
and walk humbly
with God,"[5] not being

sidetracked by resistance
nor drawn into retaliation
nor attempting to impose
self-serving human will
upon other people.

Which means transforming
one's own inner impulses
into self-sacrificial
compassion, as God's Word
and words convey.

This is a lifelong struggle
between self-preserving impulses
and trusting the transformative

---

5. Ibid., Micah 6:8b.

Spirit. Saint Paul in Romans admonishes eloquently:

"be transformed by
the renewing of your minds,
so that you may discern
what is the will of God,
what is good, and
acceptable, and perfect."[6]

---

6. Ibid., Romans 12:2.

WHAT A THERAPIST DOES

I'm at my best
as the outer ally
of your inner
spiritual quest.

It's a matter,
ultimately,
of life
and death.

At times you
want to leave me,
at other times
you need me.

Sometimes you
Want to kill me,
when your old self
doesn't want to die.

But you came
and you remain
because you
want to change.

Your vital core
needs support
to stay alive,
create a life.

The security
of the known
makes it scary
to let go.

I know it so well:
I live it myself:
the bitter and sweet;
your courage helps me.

A SPIRITUAL TEACHER

"The wind blows where it chooses,
And you hear the sound of it,
But you do not know where
It comes from, or where it goes.
So it is with everyone who
Is born of the Spirit."[1]

When Spirit appears,
One's breath knows
Immediately,
But one's mind gets it
Most clearly in hindsight,
Even if only seconds after,
leaving one breathless.

When one begins and
Continues to talk about it,
Something surges
From deep within, rising
Along the alimentary canal
In inverse direction of digestion—
A hot and molten feeling which
Leads to tears and choking
As its power overtakes one,

Like a fiery pillar
Deeply grounded
In the body's core

---

1. The Holy Bible (NRSV), John 3:18.

Conducting molten energy
Near enough the heart
To make it glow
And the lungs to quicken
With gasping breath
As the words come.

One's mind is awed, exalted,
Partaking of a wisdom
Far beyond one's ken
Yet known within—
Seeking a receptive
Respectful audience
Willing to be moved,
To have one's hair
Stand on end
As one listens
With faint then stronger
Recognition to the
Living Spirit within.

   *   *   *

I received the usual
Pre-Christmas floods of mail:
Catalogues, letters, emails—
Begging for purchases
Or year-end contributions.

I put one such letter aside
As I tried to assess

Which ones would survive the cut
Of recipients worthy of a contribution.

That letter lay there
On my computer desk
For three or four weeks
As Christmas drew nigh.

Meanwhile, into my office
Comes my Therapy patient John[2]
On his ongoing journey
Seeking mind, spirit, body unity
In his personal life, his
Relationships, and vocation,
Beset of course by doubts
And vulnerable
To quick-fix drugs and sex.

Today he gets right to it:
Says he's aware of missing
A spiritual teacher—that
He's never really had one.

I begin to feel anxious,
Yet also on alert,
Guessing that
He's coming to me for that,
Even if not consciously.

---

2. Identifying information has been changed.

I feel inadequate, thinking
It's not exactly my definition
Of what I'm about,
And wondering "Have I
Ever had a spiritual teacher?"

He's not asking me yet,
Directly, if I'll be his teacher;
Rather, he goes on to
Tell me a story of
Him and his friend enjoying
Boxing with each other.

One day while doing so,
His friend broke
A small bone in his hand.
"Immediately I felt guilty,"
John said to me, "because
Just a few days earlier
I had had the thought 'We
Should wrap our hands
Before putting on our gloves,'
But I hadn't said anything.
Now he breaks his bone!
I felt responsible."

We discussed other things
In that therapy session,
But at a timely moment
Near the end, I said,
"Back to what you said

About missing a spiritual teacher:
I'm realizing that I've never had
Only one spiritual teacher myself.
But you've gotten me thinking
That through the years,
A few key people have
Profoundly influenced me—
Both by what they said
As well as with the loving energy
With which it was conveyed
And the timing of what they said.

Those have been my spiritual teachers,
And I guess I've taken them inside—
They've become part of who I am,
And influence how I live.

You've told me about people
Like that in your life
Whom you remember,
Whose influence has helped
Things in your life to come together.

More and more over time
You can become
Your own spiritual teacher—
The more you trust
Your intuition,
The Spirit within.

Your inner teacher
Was speaking when
You had that thought
Before boxing with your friend
That you should wrap your hands.

You can increasingly
Pay attention
To those intimations."

He agreed, understood—
Heard this not as criticism
But affirmation,
As information
Which could help him
Listen to his
Inner Teacher
In the future.

We talked of other
Related things, and
As he was leaving—
While paying me
In cash as he always does—
He asked me if I
Contribute to charities.
"Yes, sure," I said.
He asked which ones.
I stumbled, said
"A couple of churches,

Other organizations
I can't recall at
The moment." I was thinking
Also it was not his business.

He intuited my discomfort,
Said immediately,
"It doesn't matter;
Would you be willing—
If I gave you an extra fifty—
To give it to a charity
Of your choosing?"

I was speechless,
Stirred deep within,
Felt Spirit moving,
Blowing.
I swallowed, choked,
Said, "Sure, I'll do that."

Yes, clinically, one could
Say that I was "enabling" him—
Doing this for him instead
Of encouraging him
To do it on his own,
To trust his inner
Spiritual Teacher.

But I sensed it was something
About our relationship that

He wanted to honor.
Autonomy would come later.

I felt deeply connected with him,
Both within, but also outside,
Beyond, or underneath
The framework of therapy.

Beyond my fee,
He was giving a gift
Both to me and through me—
Entrusting the wind which
Would blow the blessing
Where it willed, while
Giving us each a thrill.

In that spontaneous moment
His Spiritual Teacher spoke
To the One in me.
Our hearts were joined
In what transcended
The therapeutic framework
While being therapeutic.
We both were fed
And nurtured by Spirit
Within us,
Between us,
And in the room.

*   *   *

That evening at home, sitting
In front of my computer,
I suddenly saw that letter—
The one I'd left there
For three or four weeks.

It all came together!
The Spirit like the wind
Had been blowing,
Had led me to
Put that letter aside
For a time,
And in that moment
I knew that it was precisely
That Charity I was supposed
To give his money to.[3]

Which I did; and what
A fulfilling, awed,
And restful feeling of
Completion I've had.

I sent him an email
Informing him
Of the completion of
What his Spiritual Teacher
Through us both had done.

   3. Vacation From War

We'll see what happens next.
It may be mostly more
Routine, but things will
Never be the same
With him or me
Ever again.

MY MOTHER'S PAIN

I'm feeling weighed down
by my mother's pain,
which is sixty years old
but I feel the same:

a heaviness of heart,
a weightiness of limbs,
a sighing sort of breathing,
a zombyish momentum.

A deeper source of this pain
is Grandma on my mother's side,
whose lungs from seventeen
were forever compromised.

She died at sixty-one—
when I was just thirteen—
from cancer of the lungs,
a major loss for me.

Not only for who she was,
but also because my mom
depended on her so much—
was lost when she was gone.

A woman of deep Faith,
she'd raised her ten children
with never flagging love
and quiet warm devotion.

A too long-suffering wife,
with a plodding needy man,
who took all she had to give
and wanted more besides.

He moved at a snail's pace
in everything he did—
from tying his shoe laces
to getting crops planted.

Even the way he talked was
slow as blackstrap molasses;
and he swung his scythe so slowly
the weeds just stood there laughing.

"You never know, you know"
was a favorite phrase of his—
to punctuate the flow
of his absent-minded musings.

He rarely spoke to kids—
he never did to me;
as if for him they didn't exist;
but I once saw his cold cruelty.

His own son my Uncle Henry
was having an epileptic fit,
and Grandpa sat and laughed
instead of being compassionate.

In spite of his quirky ways,
he was a savvy farmer; but
incapable of warmth or praise.
His high standards never faltered.

My grandmother gave all she had,
worked herself I think to the grave;
as a way to get away from him?
What other options did she have?

I'll never forget the day
they'd gotten her diagnosis,
arrived in their car at our house,
and she and my mother collapsed

sobbing into each other's arms.
I don't even remember Grandpa;
I doubt that he knew what to do:
leave women to their emotions.

Grandma and my mother were close,
had talked every day on the phone;
when she died months later of course
my mother felt bereft and alone.

I was always a sensitive child,
highly attuned to my mother's pain.
Of her three children I was firstborn,
and my two brothers came along too soon.

Before she had children of her own,
she'd helped raise eight of her siblings;
oldest daughter though second-born of ten,
she got the love and hate mothering brings.

As a mother of her own children now,
she must have had conflicting feelings;
each son born fifteen months apart:
I picked up it was overwhelming.

As I grew older, I tried not to bother;
my Dad I'm sure reinforced that;
I recall once he tried to protect her:
told us boys, "your mom needs a break."

I remember that she had been crying,
which was alarming for us boys to see;
she'd been managing it all day after day;
we were scared of her vulnerability.

She recovered and everything went on,
which for us was certainly a relief;
but she carried a certain sadness around,
which I see now was a two-pronged grief.

She and her mother had sort of been sisters:
raising eight children with mutual support;
when Grandma died, Mom lost mother and sister,
and her own childhood had been aborted.

Her Faith which she'd learned from her parents,
and the love which she'd gotten from her mother,
sustained her amidst life's many hardships,
along with the love she shared with my father.

It took me many years to realize
that some of the pain I carried was hers;
my burden was lightened with this knowledge,
but I've had to mourn what I missed from her.

Sorting this all out is ongoing,
as is apparent in my writing this poem.
The pain was a deep bond with my mother,
but I need to let that part of her go.

DISAPPEARING NO MORE

After seeing me weekly
for seven or eight years,
she commented one day
in a wondering way—
which communicated that
it had just dawned on her:
"I don't disappear any more."

I sensed what she said
before I could integrate
the momentous impact
of this development
which had come about
so gradually in therapy
that its muted expression

inversely packed an
emotional punch
which then led to
quiet tears on
both our parts
about the healing which
had taken place.

Healing which, ironically,
led into painful feelings.
Her ability to be with them
was the healing part—

feelings too overwhelming
to have borne as a child,
teenager, and young adult.

Disappearing had become
a necessary way of coping
with her father's violent
verbal rages at her
mother, her brother,
and herself until
she became invisible:

such a good girl
as to cause no trouble:
not provoke her father;
yes attend to her mother
the way mother needed
while she herself
became a shadow.

Her mother was not
a refuge nor a comfort—
was by profession a nurse,
treated her children
in too intimate and
intrusive detail,

unconsciously
transmitted her fears
of her husband's
unpredictable rages

into her children
by heightening

their normal anxiety
about life, leaving
them no safe space
to develop
separate selves
or confidence.

Mother questioned
Patient's every decision,
and highlighted only
all the negative
possibilities that
could flow therefrom.

Patient internalized
this negative mother
in an effort to
control her influence,
but thereby ended up
second-guessing herself—

fearing and focusing
on the negative
outcomes of every
plan or aspiration
to the point of
restless anxiety,

paralysis, or even
self-sabotage, so as
to not cut off
her inner or outer
mother, whom she
tried to calm and comfort.

To no avail. Somehow,
she graduated
from Law School,
but sought therapy
at the point of facing
taking the Bar Exam.

Over the course of
our work together,
we determined that this
would have been too big a step
away from her mother
into her own identity.

She feared being alone—
with good reason,
because her mother
hadn't believed in Patient's
ability to go it on her own—
implied Patient would fail.

An additional layer of
her fear of moving on
was a fear that doing so

would leave mother alone.
Both were stuck in
Stockholm Syndrome.[1]

When she began therapy—
at the age of twenty-three—
she was obsessively studying
for the State Bar Exam,
barely containing
her underlying anxiety.

She was usually early
for her appointment,
would knock on my door,
fluttery, light on her feet,
hardly able to wait,
as if my door

was an unacceptable
boundary
separating her
from me,
and from being fed
by being with me.

After a few sessions,
she could tell, apparently,
from my facial expressions

---

1. "A condition that causes hostages to develop a psychological alliance with their captors as a survival strategy during captivity." It consists of "strong emotional ties that develop between two persons where one person intermittently harasses . . . or intimidates the other." Wikipedia, Stockholm Syndrome.

and my surprised energy,
that she was intruding.
I hadn't said anything,

but she responded by
thereafter bouncing in
a minute or two late,
thereby guaranteeing
my welcome and
avoiding interrupting me

or anxiously waiting
in the waiting room.
I came to understand—
after hearing about her
relationship with mother—
that she couldn't bear

yet another relationship
structured on another's
terms—in this case
something as seemingly
simple as the time of
her appointment.

Her job as a paralegal
paid her bills,
but was painful
because coworkers
had already
passed the Bar.

Besides, in that uncanny
way that the Spirit
invites us to grow
by placing us
in situations
or relationships

which are almost
perfect parallels
to those with parents,
thereby evoking both
conscious—and unconscious
repressed—feelings in us,

it gradually dawned
on my Patient and me
that her female boss
was an almost
uncanny clone of
Patient's mother!

This boss, Felice,
was a generation older,
generously helpful
and ostensibly
supportive of
Patient's promotion,

but then would suddenly
inversely, disproportionately
be disappointed in

Patient's performance,
and disapproving
of Patient's assertiveness—

as if Patient's
actual advancement
was a threat
to Felice's position
and identity as
the one in control.

When Patient was
down or discouraged,
Felice was warm
and reassuring,
but when Patient
was strong,

Felice would be
severely critical
of insignificant
details in Patient's
documents, and demand
that she rewrite them—

also blocking Patient's
forward momentum
by only qualifiedly
recommending her
for a long-overdue
promotion.

Yet Patient felt
dependent on Felice
and afraid to
seriously consider
leaving for a new job,
doubting she'd be hired.

This stuck-ness, too,
continued for years,
along with obsessive
preparations for—
though failing twice—
the Bar Exam.

But the new thing
was that my Patient
was expressing
in therapy
her frustration and
anger with Felice.

Expressing these feelings
about Felice, and
seeing the similarities
to her mother,
began to crack
the symbiotic egg

encasing Patient
and mother.
Patient could see

the irrationality and
self-centered orientation
and motivation of Felice,

and thus gradually
began to separate
her self-esteem
and self-worth
from what Felice
thought of her.

The relationship with me
gave her a safe place
to stand just outside
the relationships with
Felice and her mother
with diminishing guilt

as I validated her feelings
and affirmed her dawning
realization that both
of those women were
selfishly conflicted
about Patient's autonomy—

that they were hiding
their neediness behind
a guise of maternal
concern which gave them
control over their own neediness
projected into Patient;

which left Patient
doubting she could
get along without
their detailed interest,
oversight, and guidance
in all aspects of her life.

A key occurrence
which helped Patient
take yet a further
step out of dependence
on these two women
happened in therapy
and was awesome to me:

She proceeded to tell me—
as she had already told
her mother—that she
had a vaginal yeast
infection which wasn't
clearing up as quickly

as she had expected;
that she was treating it
as her doctor recommended,
but when she checked it
daily and it didn't
seem to be getting better,

she feared it was serious
and didn't know what to do.
I bracketed my sexual interest,

and hazily realized that
she was relating to herself
in the anxious, managing

way that her mother
treated her: in almost
too intimate detail.
Something inspired me
to address her anxiety,
and to say that

healing is a process:
not instantaneous,
but takes time—
as when one trusts
that a cut finger
will gradually heal:

one can just trust
that the healing is happening.
I was unaware
of the transformative
impact of my
intervention

until in the next session
she told me that
what I had said
had changed her life:
she had taken a step back
and was able to relax.

At the time, I was only
vaguely aware of the
deeper layer of what
I had said: that healing
was happening in therapy
too and could be trusted.

There was a sexual dimension
to the intimacy which
led her to want to tell me
about her vaginal infection
and at the same time
risk how I would respond.

I definitely felt
the sexual energy
and our deepening
intimacy, but maintained
the boundary and—
almost inadvertently—

my talk of trust
penetrated deeply
through multiple
layers of reality:
physical, medical,
psychological, emotional,

to the core of existence:
spiritual. Her Faith
had taken the form

mostly of assent
to propositions
and proper behavior.

The nonjudgmental
safety and acceptance
she experienced in therapy
increasingly helped her
feel loved and empowered
in her separateness.

Her Faith became more
relationship oriented—
less legalistic, moralistic;
she had more fun:
we laughed more;
she felt more mature.

She was able to end
relationships with men
who put her down
like her mother did
or were dominating, scary,
possessive like father.

She met an imperfect
but at times vulnerable
man, married him,
and had a son; and she
tried to be a different
mother than her mother.

She had gained an
individuated distance
from Felice and mother;
and felt a compassionate
love for them, even
when angry at them.

Towards father too
she gained a
greater understanding
of his frustration
in his marriage
and family of origin.

She cried when
in her own pain,
and empathized
with the pain and
defensive anger
of parents and Felice.

She was indeed
more fully present:
in her body;
with her feelings;
and in relationships—
disappearing no more.

Her journey continues:
she took a break
from studying for the Bar

in order to be present
for her son, and she's
looking for other jobs.

She's resetting
the relationship
with her mother,
Felice, and her husband
on her own terms—and
is thus more grounded;

and she is grateful to me
as someone who knows,
appreciates, and has helped her
to see her mother
and herself accurately,

which is enabling her
to be present
with her honest self
and the divine life
within her, thus
never really alone.

Later Adulthood

HOW I GOT TO KNOW MY DAD

The primary ways I got to know my father
came not from what he said about himself
nor from what he told me directly
about how he felt about me,

but from what he told me other people said,
or from what he did and how he did it.
He had exacting standards of excellence,
both as a farmer and a master wood craftsman.

He expressed his thoughtful love and care for me
by making me a striking walnut grandfather clock—
which my mother polished to a mirror finish—
as a gift upon my graduation from Theological Seminary,

and an equally exquisitely crafted walnut wall clock
when I graduated from training to be a psychotherapist.
In later years, I'd arrive home to find a surprise box
of small-scale wooden replicas of vintage automobiles,

or a variety of farm tractors, wagons, and machinery:
then a five-car wooden train set with smokestack engine,
and a wooden steam engine with remarkably intricate detail.
I treasure and display them all and always will.

With regard to revealing himself indirectly
by telling me what other people had said,
he once was visiting me when my son was a baby
who was crying restlessly after being put to bed;

after several minutes, my Dad, of course hearing this,
confided to me, "You know, Grandpa (his Dad) always said,
'A child won't go to sleep if his hands or feet are cold.'"
I checked, added a blanket, and soon not a sound was heard.

The layers of love and fatherly sensitivity
shocked me then and stay with me still:
he was passing along the love he'd received
from his father . . . to me and thence to my son.

LOVE TRAVEL

When my mother was getting to the age
when she would most likely not be able
to travel from Iowa to New Jersey again
to visit me in my new home,

my Dad was still hopeful—even though
her congestive heart failure was sapping
her energy and also contributing to
the occasional confusion of dementia—

he was still hopeful that they might make it
out East to visit me. In the way that was typical
of him putting his own emotions and wishes
in terms of what my mother wanted,

he said something I'll of course never forget—
both because of its exquisite tenderness
and its primitive elemental significance:
"A mother wants to know where her son sleeps."

They never did make it out East again,
but something about what he said
left me feeling that in a way they had:
that kind of love is what we all need.

Reflections on Art, Darkness, and Light

THE HUMAN POSITION: MADE IN THE IMAGE OF GOD

I was doing some museums in Houston,
Where Magritte's "The Human Condition"
Was hanging in the Menil Collection,
And although I thought I was visiting the painting,
It was the painting that visited me.

The painting is a painting of a
Draped window and outdoor scene
In which there is a painting
Set on an easel in front of that window,
And positioned in such a way
That the portion of the pastoral scene
Outside the window that is blocked
From view by the canvas with the painting
On it, doesn't seem blocked because
The scene outside through the window
Is painted on the canvas—
In such a way
And in such detail
That the Viewer looking
Out the window doesn't initially notice

That a portion of what one is seeing is
A painting, not the outdoors as it seems.
Yet it is and would be the outdoors
If the painting weren't there.

So what's the point of the painting,
If indeed there needs to be a point?
All I can say is that something in me
Resonated deeply. Tears welled up
Within me immediately due to an
"Aha" of recognition of something I knew
Deep inside that Magritte had captured.

I realized in a new way that
What that painting was doing—
What Magritte did in the painting—
Is the same as what the eye—
Actually the mind through the eye,
Or one could say the mind through imagination—
Does in relation to the world. Magritte
Captured something of the essence
of human "be"-ing, human existence:

Just like that painting,
We too stand between
The scene
And the seen;
Between the scene
And what we
end up seeing;

Because the mind
Through the eye
Creates what we see—
Even as the scene
Is out there.
We create, create
the world
Even as it's given to us—
Through the eye
Onto the retina
To the brain.

The artist more dramatically than the non-artist,
But every human being in fact, actively,
Actively perceives or "paints" the world—
Actively creates everything, actually.

It is the artist's, the eye's, the mind's,
The imagination's, every-human-being's
Position in the world to create the world.

I remember how fascinated I was—
Blown away even—when
I first learned in a Philosophy of Education
Class in Theological Seminary,
That the human mind, using the eye,
Actively perceives and creates
What it sees. We don't realize (except
In people whom we think of as abnormal,
Because we notice their eyes quivering)
That the eye moves microscopically back

And forth multiple times per second
As we scan and construct what we see.

Which doesn't mean that what the eye
Sees isn't there—though that may also be true,
As with a blind person or when our eyes
Are closed or we're dreaming or imagining—
But at a minimum, the mind, using the eye,
Isn't a passive screen but an active creator
Relating to what is there. It was an awesomely
Powerful way to introduce relativity—
The relativity of truth, of what we see
And know—as well as epistemology—
How we know what we know, and
Because of the subjectivity of what we see,
The importance of communicating what we see
And what we know with humility and
In consultation with community.

By painting one portion of the view
Through the window as a painting,
And in such a way that
It perfectly—well, seemingly perfectly—
Corresponds to what one sees outside
The window, Magritte brings to awareness
Not only what he as a Painter,
But also what we as humans do
All the time: actively paint a picture
Of what is outside
Through our eyes with our minds.

Which means, of course, that—
In the seeming correspondence
And congruency—there is a break:
That what an artist or human perceives
Or imagines, is a construct, a creation,
An interpretation, of "what is,"
Which also means that there's room
For variation, creativity, manipulation,
Distortion—even inversion or reversal—
In what one sees, creates, or imagines.
[With regard to inversion—
And the playful way we're made—
Neurologically the brain inverts
In a millisecond the light rays
Which enter through the eye
And are received by the retina.]

In this Magritte painting,
There seemed perfect correspondence
Between what was painted
And what was outside the window.
But part of the genius
Of the painting—part of what thrilled me
Is that my viewing of it ignited a process—
A sequence of steps, quick though they
Were—in "getting" what Magritte
Was doing or conveying. In fact, I think
He was partly conveying those very steps:

I initially saw a scene outside a draped window
Of a sky, clouds, trees, one nearer tree,
Shrubs, and grass—a beautiful view;
But I was quickly aware of the legs of an easel
In front of and below the window,
Then I saw the right side of a canvas in the view,
Then a clamp on top of the canvas holding
A painting—a painting!
Then I noticed the top and bottom edges
Of the painting, and next that the
Left edge of the painting was just a bit
Overlapping the drape on the
Left side of the window.
It was vividly clear now that
There was a painting there.[1]

As I was going through this process,
I was quietly very excited; the same way
That I remember feeling in elementary school
When I would suddenly comprehend
Something new that was being presented,
Or when I would discover
Something new to me in nature—
Like a dung beetle rolling up
then burying a ball of dung,
In which, I later learned,
It had deposited its eggs!
I was fascinated, awed, agape—
Filled with a quietly thrilled feeling.

*

1. You can Google "Rene Magritte's The Human Condition" to see the painting.

This whole sequential process
Activated my thinking,
Pondering, wondering:
What the hell is Magritte doing here?

As I said, tears welled up within me,
My heart was beating more rapidly,
And I began to grasp that this painting
Was speaking to me with the voice of
Its own authority about what it's like
To be an artist, and more universally,
A human being in relation to the world.

This process of comprehending the Painting
Began when I was viewing it, but continued
Afterwards as I kept contemplating and
Integrating the glowing fire of growing insight
Ignited within me by the painting.

But the deepest layer of resonance
That I sensed at the time
But only later began
to conceptualize,
Constellate, articulate,
Is that we human beings as human beings
In all our creative and destructive potential,
In this very way are—how can I say it—
Images of God!
God as Creator!

We stand
> Between

God
> And the world:

We are both divine and human!
God lives in our bodies,
And has made our minds
Creative, just like God's Spirit
Brooding over the face of the waters,[2]
Bringing order out of chaos.

Like God, we create
Or "paint" the world;
But more than that,
Our very beings—
Who we are,
How we live—
Are "paintings" by God
And of God:
We represent life
As lived alienated from God,
Or life as constructive,
Merciful, compassionate,
And partnered with God.

Either way, the "painting"
Of each human life reveals
The consequences in
Each person's way of living

---

2. The Holy Bible (NRSV), Genesis 1:2.

Of each person's connection
Or lack thereof with
Spiritual reality.

We all—not only Jesus—
Are both Spirit and flesh:
Bodies alive by Spirit,
We are creative persons,
Images, representations,
"Paintings," of God
Or the absence of God.

It's true that Jesus
Lived out more fully
Than anyone else
Divine love and will,
Divine presence incarnate;
That's why Jesus is called
The Word of God.
But we are all
Images of God.
We too can be
Words of God.

God is both in the world
And creating—and letting die—
The world: Spirit in substance,
Dust alive with Spirit—
As revealed in scripture
And most clearly in Jesus,

The living Word of God
(As distinct from the written word).

In other words, not only perceptually
And epistemologically, but also spiritually,
We are like that Painting: an expression,
Or intermediary, or representation of
That Spirit/spiritual Life-energy
That created and sustains
The entire universe.

We stand, exist, "be" in the world
In the same way that Magritte's painting does:
In-between Creator-Spirit and world;
We partake of both
Spirit and world.

Jesus leaves us with the
Sacrament of Eucharist
To regularly remind us
That just like he was,
We too are Spirit-bodies:
We re-member, remind
Ourselves that we are
Broken and dying but
Incarnate Holy Spirit.

By ingesting
Bread and wine,
Body and blood,
We take into ourselves

The life-giving substance
Of God who was incarnate
In Jesus as The Way,
The Truth, and The Life,
Thereby strengthening ourselves
spiritually to live
And die as Jesus did.

Our lives can be sacraments,
Evidence of divine presence
In all of human experience,
Including death.

Just as paint
Is comprised of
Earthy substance
Arranged by the painter
To exist on a canvas,

So also humans
Are shaped of dust
By the Creator, and
Enlivened to exist
By Spirit-breath.

Spirit and material substance
Unite and exist both
Within us and outside us.

As human beings—
As bodies and minds
Alive with Spirit-breath—
We are conscious, intentional
Creatures who by virtue of
The way we're built and wired,
Are always creating the world,
And as we mature and
Gain spiritual awareness,
We increasingly consciously
Shape and direct our own
Identity—our selves—
And the world we inhabit.
We become increasingly aware
That we're responsible
For who we are
And how we live.

This responsibility is almost
Too much to realize, to tolerate—
Which may be why we don't think
Too much about it.

We're active intermediaries of the Divine Presence
Which inhabits and undergirds the universe:
Of that Spirit which is the source
Of human life and all life,
Which lives and breathes in us
In bodily form until the death
Of body and other forms,
Whereupon the Spirit creates

New forms and bodies to inhabit
For a time.
Eternity in time.

It's weighty, sobering, thrilling,
To realize that we are responsible
For the degree to which our identity—
As well as the world which
We perceive, inhabit, and create—
Correspond to who God is
And what God is about.

The medium is our bodies and minds,
The canvas is our lives—a frieze,
Freeze, cross-section,
Of the way we live
At any given moment in time.
We are paintings, canvases
Corresponding more or less
To God's presence in this world.

Our creativity and responsibility
Are given us by the Creator Spirit
Who created us in God's image
And invites us, wants us
To be partners and co-creators
Of our identities and the world.

What an awesome and thrilling responsibility!
The challenge of course is to do this

With humility and in concert with all
The rest of humanity and the non-human world.
Humans can consciously seek to discern
The will of the Great Spirit,
And seek to create a "painting," a self,
A life, and a world, which corresponds
As closely as possible with that Great Spirit's
Will for the Universe, or not.

When saying that only Jesus was fully
Divine and fully human, Christians
Run the risk of abnegating each person's
Responsibility to embody and
Bear witness to the divine presence
In each of us and in the world,
To live justly, love mercy,
And walk humbly with God.[3]

There's much that we don't understand,
That we fear and don't want to accept:
Sickness, violence, suffering, death.
But even amidst all this darkness,
God wants us to be
Thoughtful co-creators of new life
And new ways of "be-"ing.

We're free to go our own way.

When we choose
Correspondence or harmony,

3. Ibid., Micah 6:8.

It results in a deep inner and
Outer peace and joy which undergirds
Even the anxiety of change, tumult,
Sickness, decay, disaster, and death.

Things can go horribly awry
When humans ignore or defy
The Spirit's presence and desire,
Choosing instead to live
In a deluded pride
Which believes that
We, apart from Spirit,
Know what's best.

True, even at our best,
When we want to live
In accord with divine will—
Rather than seek security
Through our own efforts—
It's a lifelong process.

There is an everyday struggle
Between human will and divine will.
As the apostle Paul puts it,
"I do not do what I want,
But I do the very thing I hate."[4]
"Wretched man that I am."[5]
But thank God that Jesus
As Word shows us the way.[6]

    4. Ibid., Romans 7:15.
    5. Ibid., 7:24.
    6. Ibid., 7:25.

When we try to live as Jesus did,
The Spirit of God dwells in us;[7]
And all who are led
By the Spirit of God
Are children of God.[8]

Living as led by Spirit
Does involve sacrifice
Of our human will.
St. Paul continues:
"I appeal to you
Brothers and sisters,
By the mercies of God,
To present your bodies
As a living sacrifice,
Holy and acceptable to God,
Which [kind of living] is
Your spiritual worship."[9]

He urges further: "Do not
Be conformed to this world,
But be transformed
By the renewing of your minds,
So that you may discern
What is the will of God—
What is good and acceptable
And perfect."[10]

---

7. Ibid., 8:9
8. Ibid., 8:14.
9. Ibid., 12:1.
10. Ibid., 12:2.

Paul adds elsewhere
"Do you not know
That you are God's temple,
And that God's Spirit dwells in you?"
"For God's temple is holy,
And you are that temple."[11]

The writer of the Gospel
According to John addresses this
When he quotes Jesus as saying,
"I have come down from heaven,
Not to do my own will,
But the will of him who sent me."[12]
"Whoever has seen me
Has seen the Father."[13]
"The words that I say to you
I do not speak on my own;
But the Father who dwells
In me does his works."[14]

Any human being
And every other created thing
Is temporal and finite;
But any human alive
Is a living being
Enlivened by creative Spirit,
And as such is made

11. Ibid., I Corinthians 3:16, 17b.
12. Ibid., John 6:38
13. Ibid., 14:9c
14. Ibid., 14:10 b– c.

In the image of God,
And more or less accurately
Represents or images
Divine presence and will.

Just as an artist
Sometimes starts over,
Or even paints overtop of
An existing painting,
So we too can change
Our identity so that
It more accurately
Represents the divine
Will for who we can be
And how we live.

When thus aligned,
People seeing me
Will see a "painting"
That closely corresponds
To the otherwise invisible
Or hidden presence
Of spiritual reality
"Behind" the "painting"
That is me,
A Spiritual "kingdom"
Alive in me and
Transparently shining
Through me.

This Magritte painting
Captured for me
The human position:
Made in God's image;
And evoked in me a resonance
With the deeper layers
Of Divine Presence—
Within us and all around us.

My synapses then as now
Were exploding like fireworks,
Making my heart pound
And my breath quicken.

I now understand the phrase
"In the image of God
[God] created them,"[15]
In an entirely new way,
As well as the words
With which both Jesus
And John the Baptist
Began their ministry:
"Repent,
For the kingdom of heaven
Is at hand." [16] That is,
Be penitent again:
Remember your humble position
In relationship with God.

---

15. Ibid., Genesis 1:27b.
16. Ibid., Matthew 3:2.

The Divine Spirit
May be seen
Living in us
And through us,
For God's sake!

VELASQUEZ' ADORATION OF THE MAGI

So many famous paintings
in the Prado in Madrid.
Little did I know
which one would reach me.

It was Diego Velasquez'
Adoration of the Magi[1]
which caught my eye,
but even more deeply
my awe, at the intimacy
of the scene. Immediately
I was with the three wise men
Adoring the baby Jesus.

The story is so familiar
we don't stop to wonder:
why adore this baby?
The particular episode
portrayed in this painting
is but one part
of a story which
developed out of a
"divined" mystery
in the universe.
And there he sits,
being adored.

---

1. A photo of the painting can be viewed by googling: "Velasquez' Adoration of the Magi."

The story believes
That this baby Jesus is
Divinity in human flesh—
from the time of conception
to birth and death.
The miracle
of the biological process
of birth itself
is but one layer
of mystery inhering here.

The bright bold colors
highlight this layer
of childhood as miraculous,
but the Viewer is drawn deeper
by the contrast between
light on the child and the
darkness of the surround.

I was already drawn in,
but then when I read
that Velasquez had
painted his own family
as the Holy Family,
my mind was blown.

I was touched to tears,
and to writing this poem—
thrilled at what the Artist
in Velasquez had done:

the Artist himself as
one of the wise men,
his wife as the Virgin Mary,
and their daughter
as the baby Jesus!

When I recovered
and could think again,
his audacity struck me dumb!
Was this an exercise in
heretical reductionism?
grandiose narcissism?
ironical cynicism?

But no, creative genius!
In doing this, Velasquez
had brought the mystery
of the incarnation—
Spirit inhabiting flesh—
arrestingly into the present:
relevant to him,
his family, his era,
and now also to me,
to us, to any viewer
throughout history.

Whether intentional or not,
the artist Velasquez himself
in this painting
performed a miracle.

The painting is not only
about past history
but present mystery!
The characters in the work
are not simply sitters
in yet another rendering
of a Christian theme,
but active participants
in Divine presence.

The audacious thing
that Velasquez did
is to posit his child
as the Christ child.
Consciously or not
his work declared
that all human beings—
beginning at conception
and miraculously birthed—
are children of God.

Such a realization—
courageous assertion—
makes it more difficult
for us or anyone
to place the miracle
of God-within-us
into the distant past
and into only the
one human, Jesus.

I want to think
that Velasquez is saying,
"Wow, divine life
is in my child too—
as well as in Jesus,
as the Jesus story tells me—
and I'm on my knees
worshipping the awesome
presence of Divine Life
in my child!
And I hope that
this awareness influences
the ways I relate to
this child, my child,
each child, as well as myself
and all human beings:
we're sacred beings
full of Divine Life!"
That's the whole point
Of the Christmas story,
the Jesus Story,
is it not?
God is with us,
Spirit enfleshed,
God in us!

Either Velasquez,
or the Artist in him,
or both, got it!
He got it
and he painted it!

And what better posture
for himself in the painting
but to be kneeling in awe,
showing us viewers how to be
in the presence of mystery.

REMBRANDT'S JUDAS[1]

Prostrate and twisted
he half sits, half lies
at the feet of
the tall chief priest
and haughty scribes—
one of whom is
turning his head away
as if in disgust and
gesturing backwards
with his hand as if
to tell Judas to get away
as one would to a dog.

On the back and side
of Judas' head
are small red spots—
sores caused by his
having pulled out
his hair
in anguish
by the roots.

To Judas' left
a man sits
not looking at him
and with his back
to the viewer.

1. To see the painting, google "Judas Returning the Thirty Pieces of Silver" by Rembrandt.

Behind him and
on the floor
to Judas' left
are pieces of silver—

thirty to be exact—
which he's thrown there,
returning in full
the payment he received
for his betrayal of Jesus.

Clearly he's repented
of his contractual deed,
though too late to change
the course of events.

The viewer aches for him
in his desperation,
aches the more so
seeing the scorn and
blatantly-turned backs
of those to whom
Judas turns
for absolution.

Rembrandt may be
holding the viewer there
to share the agony of him
who has turned again
for the second time
to the wrong people
for help.

These religious authorities'
hearts are smugly dead,
confronted now however
with how to proceed
with this unexpected twist
in their deadly plot.

They whored Judas
for their own ends;
now consider him
a pathetic nobody
whom they wish
would go away.

We see clearly here
the heart of each
character, and we fear
no way out
other than the suicide
with which we know
the story ends.

*   *   *

Rembrandt's "Judas
Returning the Thirty
Pieces of Silver"
is considered his
first masterpiece.
Again the theme
of light and dark—

brilliant light
in the darkness
of the surround
shining on the scriptures
open to the page
in the book of Matthew[2]
telling the story which
Rembrandt here paints.

There's enough light
to see Judas' face
and a spot of light
on the sleeve of
the rejecting hand—
perhaps to draw
inescapable attention
to the centrality
of this cold-hearted act.

Interesting that Judas
turned to them.
In his doing so,
there was a chance
they all could have
been redeemed:
the light was there,
but . . . .

*   *   *

---

2. The Holy Bible, Matthew 27:3–10

Readers of the Gospel narrative
know that the other eleven
disciples are elsewhere,
full of fear, but together,

dealing with their
own deepest doubts—
personified in the one
known forever after
as Doubting Thomas:
there was room
in their midst for him.

Would there have been
room for a betrayer?
Yes, because they
were already there:
Peter had denied
knowing Jesus, and
all the others
had fled at the
presence of danger—
betrayers all.

Judas isolated himself
from the one group
who could have
probably forgiven him.

He had repented for
betraying innocent blood;

was having trouble
forgiving himself;
sought absolution.
But turned for the
second time to those
who'd never give it.

How close he came!
His brothers could have
shared his shame.
But in the end
he couldn't break free
from the old religion
and its leaders.

He was strangely
still attached to them
even via the money,
even though trying
to break free of it
by returning it to them,
perhaps hoping
to undo his deed,
or hoping they would
change their minds,

perhaps not fully
realizing until they
rejected the money
as well as him
how insignificant

and powerless he was
now to alter
the course of events.

He had felt important
when the Establishment
wanted information
from him: easy then
for him to confuse
his value with money value,
and he must then
have unthinkingly assumed
that he still had power
by returning the money.

When the money was rejected
and he was dismissed
and even scorned,
he then no doubt felt
that he had no value
and that this was
indeed the end for him:
that he may as well be dead—
that ending his life
was the one thing
still in his power
to accomplish.[3]

His going back to
the established religion

3. Ibid.

leads one to think
that even deeper
than any regrets,
deeper than repentance,
lay wounded pride—

his center of gravity
was still stuck in his ego
rather than in sobbing
the way that Peter did
after thrice denying Jesus.
Peter thus showed that he
was still profoundly
connected to Jesus,
and thus to the
forgiving, life-giving
Spirit that changed him
and could have
changed Judas
and restored him
to a relationship with
Jesus, the Holy Spirit,
and the other disciples
had he died to his
self-centered ego
and sought new life
in serving that Power
beyond self-interest.

Tragic indeed was his end:
money-man to the end:
he couldn't get beyond

himself and his shiny coins.
The light lay outside
not within him.

    *   *   *

Why would Rembrandt
paint this scene?
What's to be gained?
The answer lies—
as in most art—
with whether or not
we see ourselves
in the painting—
even in a painting
as dark as this one.

In the light of this
mostly dark painting,
Rembrandt invites the viewer
to see oneself:
to see in oneself
the pride of Judas
trying to control events;
and to see the darkness
in ourselves which—
like the Establishment—
would self-righteously
turn our backs
on frightened, desperate
people like Judas.

It's scary and sobering
to see how, even though
Judas had lost almost
everything, in the end
he couldn't or wouldn't
let in the light of new life.

He'd been exposed
to that life in Jesus
and the other disciples
but hadn't learned
to surrender his will
to the will of transcendent
Spirit with which
Jesus was so intimate,
as to call It "Papa."

Jesus saw the light
of that Spirit-world
near at hand
and within himself.
He also shared
his inner struggles
between his will
and divine will—
teaching that the cost
would be death,
but a death revealing
the Spirit's presence,
and also how to die—

that when facing death,
one could speak about
or envision a life
beyond material life
and a power greater
than human power;

that one could demonstrate—
as did John the Baptist[4]—
that one's ultimate loyalty
was to Spirit-power,
not to any human power.

It's in that loyalty
and the fellowship
it creates
that true life lies—
before and after death.

It's scary to see
how hard it can be
to trust the light within us
and follow where it leads us:
because it will illuminate
and confront our pride;
reveal the darkness
in our hearts; and
call us to change
our willful ways—

---

4. The Holy Bible (NRSV), Matthew 14:1–12; Mark 6:14–29; Luke 9:7–9.

our subtle avoidance
of the pain and shame
we'll have to endure
as we slowly mature
into Spirit-led people
who live new lives.

Judas came so close:
he sought forgiveness,
but, alas, he sought it
from the treacherous ones
who were opposed to Jesus
and the Holy Spirit.

What about us?
how often do we
reject the light
inside ourselves or
outside, beckoning us
or lighting our way;
betray it out of fear;
manipulate events
to avoid surrender
to Spirit-guidance;
turn our haughty backs
on those seeking help?

When we veer off course
do we at times also
think of ourselves
as pathetic, hopeless,

beyond redemption;
think that death is
the only way out?
Do we get stuck
in old structures
and identities,
turn to the wrong
people for help?

Judas in the end
turned his own back
on himself, as well as on
the Spirit which would
have helped him forgive
himself and find new life.

But the Gospel writer
didn't forget Judas
or the Judas in us;
neither did Rembrandt.

ASK ANYTHING

At the Food Court with his grandson,
Tim had a low-grade worry
that seven-year-old Jeff
could at any time have an angry outburst
at any provocation big or small.

They'd been having an okay time
wandering the mall, which Jeff loved,
but sure enough, he didn't like
the pizza he had said he wanted, and
when Tim said, "Just eat it, Jeff,"

he banged his fist on the table,
said "No," got up, and stomped off.
"Here we go," thought Tim, getting up
and calling, "Jeff, stop, come on back."
Jeff kept going. Long-legged Tim, in pursuit,

caught him from behind by the shoulders,
saying "Jeff, stop; come on back, listen to me."
Jeff tried to wrench free,
so Tim reached around him from behind and
grabbed Jeff's wrists tightly across in front of Jeff,

as if putting him in human straightjacket.
Immediately Jeff began thrashing and
twisting with a violent angry energy,
trying to escape his Grandpa's grasp,
kicking backwards against Tim's shins,

stomping on Tim's toes, banging the back
of his head against Tim's upper chest
and chin, cutting Tim's inner lip on his teeth.
Tim was amazed at Jeff's strength, and
was trying to not get violent himself,

saying "Jeff, stop. Calm down. Stop, Jeff!"
To no avail, and Tim was beginning to tire,
wondering "What if I can't hold him?"
People were now staring at them, wondering—
Tim feared—who's the problem here?

At that moment the words came to Tim,
"If you ask anything in my name, I will do it."[1]
"Help me, Jesus," Tim prayed out loud,
"Jesus, please help me; help me Jesus!"
Immediately Jeff calmed down.

To this day, Tim can and can't believe it.
A man of deep faith and prayer,
he also knows the Bible inside and out.
Not fully shocked therefore at what happened,
he was at the same time completely shocked

that the power he called upon worked
so dramatically. Jeff relented, relaxed.
Tim released him, and Jeff went over
and sat on a bench along the wall,
where Tim joined him—both exhausted.

1. The Holy Bible (RSV), John 14:14.

This has echoes of the gospel story
summarizing Jesus' healing
of the man possessed by demons, who was
unable to be restrained, but who afterwards
was sitting clothed and in his right mind.[2]

Tim believes the kingdom of heaven
is at hand—a reality within us
and around us, preceding and defying
human understanding, even as we
in response try to understand it:

Something about opening one's eyes,
being aware of a spiritual dimension,
something about asking and receiving,
about seeking and finding,[3] about
God is love—healing body, mind, spirit—

sometimes dramatically, sometimes gradually.
Did Jeff perhaps feel non-punitively and
securely held—physically and spiritually—
as his Grandpa held him and prayed—
allowing Jeff to feel calm deep inside?

Like Jacob of old, Jeff also
engaged in an exhaustive battle
over who's ultimately in charge,
whom to trust—himself alone,
or a higher authority, whom

---

2. Ibid.(NRSV), Mark 5:1–20.
3. Ibid., Matthew 7:7.

he willfully resisted surrendering to?
But such willfulness cripples a person,
so Jacob had to acknowledge that there
was a Power greater than himself,
which, if he relented, would bless him.

God did bless Jacob, and gave him
a new name, which acknowledged
Jacob's strength while at the same time
placed his strength in the context
of a mutually vulnerable relationship.[4]

Tim experienced Jeff's strength,
as well his own vulnerability
in the face of Jeff's willfulness,
and knew he needed to call on
a Power greater than both of them.

Tim's faith made that divine presence
real in that moment as he invoked it.
And for Jeff, hearing his Grandpa pray,
snapped him out of "me-versus-him," and who wins,
and enabled him to feel undergirding Love.

As early as two years of age,
humans begin to struggle with
parents over who's in charge—
gradually coming to terms
with their own power and its limits,

---

4. Ibid, Genesis 32:22‑32.

as well as their ultimate
vulnerability and dependency—
even as they become more independent.
Jacob learns that it's not who wins,
but underlying love that really matters.

When held securely within loving,
non-retaliatory, nonviolent limits
by an adult similarly containing himself,
Jeff could still be himself
and be neither too powerful nor isolated.

After his midnight wrestling, Jacob
is snapped out of his expected
violent battle with his brother Esau,
and is more open to the astonishing
love and forgiveness Esau presents![5]

"If you ask anything in my name,
I will do it."[6]

---

5. Ibid., 33:1–17.
6. Ibid., John 14:14.

THE ABYSS

What is this abyss
which I dance
on the precipice of?

Breathless with fear,
I'm there or nearing it
without wanting to be:

a vast nothingness
in the face of which
I think I want death.

It's hard to imagine
moving on calmly
day to day after this.

I wonder "Is this a taste
of what Jesus experienced
on the cross, when, dying

he cried with a loud voice,
"My God, my God, why
have you forsaken me?"[1]

A daunting abyss
he was facing,
hauntingly alone.

---

1. The Holy Bible, Mattthew 27:46b.

But he's addressing God!
Quoting scripture![2]
Does this fit together?

Minutes later, he's
crying with a loud voice,
"Father, into your hands

I commend my spirit.
Having said this,
He breathed his last."[3]

When I startle awake
at three or four a.m.,
hyperventilating—

my diaphragm
not dropping down
so I can breathe,

my mind kicks in;
I begin to think, and
Scripture comes to me.

My mind reminds me
this is a Spirit thing,
and I recite a hymn:

---

2. Ibid., Psalm 22:1–2.
3. Ibid., Luke 23:46.

"Breathe on me, breath of God,
Fill me with life anew;
That I may love

What Thou dost love,
And do what Thou wouldst do.
Breathe on me breath of God,

Till I am wholly Thine;
Until this earthly part of me
Glows with Thy fire divine."[4]

* * *

"Nothingness" terrifies me
until I begin to see that in that
"nothing" is the unborn me.

"In the beginning . . . the earth
was a formless void
and darkness covered

the face of the deep
while a wind from God
swept over the face of the waters."[5]

The "deep" has a face!
And a "wind from God"
brushes over that face,

---

4. Hatch, Edwin, "Breath on Me, Breath of God," #316, in The Presbyterian Hymnal. Louisville, Kentucky, Westminster/John Knox Press, 1990.

5. Ibid., Genesis 1:1a; 2.

whereupon God creates!

In that context—darkness
and a formless void—
God creates:

everything in the world!
Animate, inanimate,
in intricate detail;

forms my inward parts;
knits me together in
my mother's womb.[6]

Breathes into me
the breath of life!
Remembering all this,

I begin to relax,
slowly surrender
to a Being

with awesome energy
without whose indwelling
I would not be.

God created me
to be awake
and to sleep

---

6. Ibid., Psalm 139:13.

in daily rhythm
harmonious with
light and darkness.

   *   *   *

But I worry:
what do I do,
what's the future?

How do I fill
the empty spaces
of hours and days?

"... Can any of you
by worrying add
a single hour

to your span of life,"
Jesus asks. "Do not
worry about tomorrow."[7]

Will this comfort me?
Not easily.
But as I breathe

and remember
those persons
who've comforted me,

---

7. Ibid., Matthew 6:27, 34.

or who've shown
or talked of
being helped

by prayer
or other ways
of being connected

to Spirit's presence,
I begin to pray too,
for others and for me.

I gradually calm down
as I realize that
I'm part of "so great

a cloud of witnesses,"[8]
whose witness helps me
"not to lose heart."[9]

I'd be alone indeed
without these scriptures
and Healers who remind me

that "nothingness"—
though usually scary—
is the amniotic air

8. Ibid., Hebrews 12:1.
9. Ibid., 12:5.

in which God creates,
posits, places me—
infinitesimal me,

who when I'm in tune,
am a body, mind, spirit
with God's creativity.

     *   *   *

Speaking of his own journey,
my Uncle Alan
recently reminded me

of the words of God
spoken through Isaiah
to us "rebellious people,

faithless children . . .
who will not hear
the instruction of the Lord;

. . . thus said the Lord God,
the Holy One:
'In returning and rest

you shall be saved;
in quietness and trust
shall be your strength.'"[10]

 10. Ibid., Isaiah 30:9,15.

". . . the Lord waits
to be gracious to you;
. . . he will rise up

to show mercy to you.
. . . blessed are all those
who wait for him."[11]

With a shock of insight
that just came to me
while writing this poem,

I realize that "waiting"
is by definition
temporal,

a way of being in time—
is actually an active way
of passing time. . . .

Waiting for God—
who is waiting for me—
is purposeful,

anticipatory,
hopeful,
relational;

---

11. Ibid., 30:18.

gives meaning to
my life, my days,
time passing,

and beckons me
to meet God
unashamed,[12]

living out the mercy,
love, and compassion
which God shows me.

With these reminders,
I wait for God,
find God waiting for me—

actually alive in me—
inspiring me to arise with God
and resume daily activities.

---

12. Ibid., Hebrews 11:2b.

WHAT'S IN A FACE?*

I recently saw the movie *Samsara*,
And was amazed at the extreme
Variations in the shape and
Features of the human faces
Of people around the world.

Which led me to think again
About the relativity of beauty—
About how someone whom I
Would consider unattractive—
And they me, no doubt—

Is the object of passionate,
Erotic, or familial love and
Adoration—even veneration.
So what is it about a face
That has universal appeal,

No matter the visible variations?
En route to understanding this,
Let me ask if you've ever noticed
The striking resemblance in features
Or profiles of partnered couples?

Until very recently, I assumed
That this was essentially narcissism:
That an individual is enchanted
By his/her own face and is thus
Drawn to the similar face of another.

Then at a psychoanalytic conference,
I was reminded by a Presenter[1]
Of the dramatic response of an infant
To the showing up of its mother's face:
The infant smiles in animated response

With equal or even greater intensity
To the mother's face than
To mother's nurturing breast.
(Breast-feeding of course includes both
Visual and physical contact.)

Studies have shown that
A baby is born prepared to see
The mother's interested face.[2]
The baby is hard-wired to respond
To the mother's face; but the new

Idea that really excited me
Is that the interested, attentive,
Engaging face of mother
Is the prototype of beauty
For that particular child.

The idea or concept of beauty, then,
Originates at the beginnings of life!

    1. From a Conference Talk entitled "Beauty and the Idea" by Arlene Kramer Richards.
    2. Spitz, Rene, First Year of Life. International Universities Press, 1966. Beebe, Beatrice, and Frank Lachmann,
    Beebe and Lachmann, The Origins of Attachment: Infant Research and Adult Treatment. Routledge, 2013.

The mother's face is the primary
Locus of focus in the mother-infant
Relationship. The mouth erotically

Ingests food, and the eye-contact
Orients the baby in space and time.
Hopefully the ongoing relationship
Is embued with enough love
That the infant feels held

Securely enough both physically
And emotionally to be able to optimally
Tolerate the inevitable maternal
Failures in empathic attunement,
Feeding, and cleaning ministrations.

The good-enough mother both awaits
The infant's signals of need or distress
And also responds in a timely enough
Manner which helps the baby tolerate
Frustration and live in hope.

But a consistent variable
In the infant's life is mother's face—
Even when the baby may turn away
From mother's face when satiated
Or disappointed or needs a break.[3]

But I'm reviewing all this
To say that I arrived at a deeper

---

3. Ibid., Beebe and Lachmann.

Understanding of what's in a face
After being exposed to that connection
Between beauty and the mother's face.

Beauty is of course then relative,
But the reason an individual
Is drawn to a face resembling
One's own is not simply narcissism,
But, more deeply, that one's own face

Resembles that of mother as beauty—
Mother as the specific definition
And image of beauty. But then it's
Not the reflection of one's own face
That one is most deeply drawn to;

Rather, one sees in the face of the partner
Some resemblance to mother,
Whom oneself would also resemble
In some features, but one's love
Isn't simply self-love, but love of other—

Originally mother, which makes for
An interpersonal relationship—
Grounded in early symbiosis with mother
But including the journey to separate
Personhood—which values self and other.

What's in a face, then,
Is not simply narcissistic

Self-love and self-reflection,
But the prototype of beauty
And—mostly—relationship.

The more one thinks about it,
"Face" takes on the quality
Of metaphor. Which is possible
Because the literal face
Is so multifaceted.

As the interface between
Two separate people,
The face is a central
Vehicle of communicating
So much that humans feel—

A supercharged vehicle,
Because the emotions may
Be displayed on the face
Directly from the amygdala,[4]
Sometimes before one thinks.

Neurologically wired this way,
The face can give nuanced
And exquisite expression
To what a person is feeling
Before conscious intention.

But the face is only one

---

4. The amygdala is that part of the human brain which "performs a primary role in the processing of memory, *decision-making*, and *emotional reactions*." [Wikipedia]

Vehicle of communication;
And even wired as it is,
It can be rife with deception,
And used for manipulation.

For as much as it reveals,
A face also conceals much
Of what a person at any
Given moment is experiencing
Or feeling or thinking.

This is due to the complexity
Which arises from the fact that
The person may be simultaneously
Thinking about what she or he
Is feeling and experiencing,

Therefore also making choices
About what to express, what to
Conceal, what to repress;
Not to mention that one has
Contradictory feelings all at once.

It's understandable then that
We think of "face" as metaphor;
Even more importantly so
Because there's much more
To communication than what

We can see or express via face.
Hugely significant is the voice—

And of that, the tone, volume,
Cadence, modulation—plus
The reality and quality of touch.

Beyond even all of this, there's
A sense of Presence, inner space,
Which exists within and behind
The face, but also transcends it.
Thus the face begins to represent

A fascinating boundary between
One person and another,
Between inner and outer—
That which connects while
At the same time separates:

The face is like a veil—a gauze
Which activates a teasing
Interplay between known
And unknown, between
Fear and fascination:

Bordering on mystery—
That which can't be fully known
But compellingly glimpsed.
Also in this territory resides Spirit,
As well as sacred scripture, which is

Another interface—in this case,
Between human and Spirit.

Scripture plays extensively with
"Face" as a metaphor of Divine
Presence and relationship.

When Cain—after killing Abel
His brother due to envy over
Abel's favorable relationship
With God—was banished by
God from tilling the soil, (and

Cain loved the soil), he said to God,[5]
"My punishment is greater than
I can bear; today you have
Driven me away from the soil, and
I shall be hidden from your face."[6]

These archetypal stories about God
Are the ancient Hebrews' creative
Ways of articulating, dramatizing,
And validating internal experiences
Of transcendent spiritual presence.

With a great deal of respect and caution,
This spirit within is called JHVH [God],
Conceptualized in human terms
As a divine personage with a face,
With whom one has a relationship.

This story about Cain and Abel hints at

5. The Holy Bible (NRSV), Genesis 4:1–12.
6. Ibid., 4:13–14.

The existence—or lack thereof—of an inner
Alignment between a person's ways
Of living and relating, and how the
Spirit within wants them to be.

Note the link in this story
Between "face" and "presence."
Cain's deepest fear is God's
Withdrawal and absence.
It's a touching narrative:

As soon as Cain cries out
To God, God immediately
Promises to protect Cain
From further human revenge.[7]
No capital punishment here.

But it's saddening to read
That "Cain went away from
The presence of the Lord."[8]
In the end, Cain drifts away
From God, lives as a fugitive.

Psychologically, of course, this
Interaction between God and Cain
Can be understood as an
Internal drama within Cain
After he killed his brother:

He felt so appalled and
Estranged from his spiritual

---

7. Ibid., 4:15.
8. Ibid., 4:16a.

Core that he definitely couldn't
Be at peace with himself;
Thus became a wanderer.

These stories teach that
Even amidst changing ways of life—
From Abel as hunter-gatherer to
Cain as a settled farmer—
Humans can be nonviolent siblings.

The fact that a face both reveals
And conceals is dealt with
Exquisitely in the biblical stories
About the intimate relationship
Between God and Moses.

On the one hand, we read that
When Moses asks for greater
Self-disclosure of Godself,
God stammers about what God
Will do and give, but concludes,

"You cannot see my face, for
No one shall see me and live."[9]
Touchingly, God wants to reveal
More, so tells Moses to carefully
Position himself in a cleft of rock

Where God will cover Moses
With his hand while God passes by

9. Ibid., Exodus 33:17–21.

In all God's substantial fullness;
Then, God says, "I will take away
My hand, and you will see my back,

But my face shall not be seen."[10]
Such heart-thrilling interplay
Between being seen and not-seen;
All in the context of Moses going
Alone into the Tent of Meeting,

Where, we read, "the Lord
Used to speak to Moses face to
Face, as one speaks to a friend":[11]
Seemingly contradictory depictions
Of God and Moses' relationship.

Which one is true?
Both, we can say.
Together they capture
The paradox of intimacy,
And the need for a boundary.

So much can be known;
People can become so close;
Yet there's always more
To each person's wholeness
Than can be fully known

Until, as Saint Paul writes,
We die: "Now we see

10. Ibid., 33:21–23.
11. Ibid., 33:7–11a.

In a mirror, dimly, then
We will see face to face."[12]
This helps us make sense

Of those several scripture
Passages dealing with Divine-
Human relationships
In which the person is amazed
If she/he sees God's face and lives.

Survival of that degree
Of intimacy between God and
A particular human is due
To God's grace, protection, and
Giving the person a mission.

When the angel of the Lord
Appears to Gideon while he's
Beating wheat in the wine press,
The angel greets him saying,
"The Lord is with you, mighty warrior."

The angel ignores Gideon's doubts
And complaints about God's absence,
Stays on theme, turns to face him—
Then suddenly it's "The Lord"—
Saying, "Go in this might of yours

And deliver Israel from Midian;

---

12. Ibid., I Corinthians 13:12.

I hereby commission you." [13]
In ongoing disbelief, Gideon
Seeks proof that it's God speaking,
Which he eventually receives;

Whereupon he cries out "Help me,
Lord, for I have seen the angel
Of the Lord face to face."
The Lord replies, "Peace be to you;
Do not fear, you shall not die."[14]

Un-boundaried intimacy
Is in fact hard to imagine,
If not actually impossible
With each person remaining
Alive as a separate person;

Each individual
Needs his/her own center
Of autonomy and authority,
And from that inner place
He/she is free to choose

For or against the intimacy,
And how close to be.
Mutual autonomy and
Respectful intimacy
Are difficult to achieve.

God does not wish to

13. Ibid., Judges 6:11–14.
14. Ibid., 6:22–23.

Annul human autonomy;
Rather seeks to model
In presence and epiphany
How to live in harmony:

There's an emotional charge,
An intensity, longing—
Even sexual energy—
In the conversational
Dance of intimacy—

With which we can identify—
In the interaction
Between God and Moses:
The imagery of clefts
And backs, seeing, not seeing.

Sexual energy in the context
Of Spirituality gives added and
Enhanced depth, tension, and
Dimension to each one—transcendent
Life energy in and between bodies!

As in any relationship,
the one with God, too,
Includes presence and
Absence—sometimes mutual,
Other times against one's will,

Leaving one feeling abandoned,

Wondering if forgotten,
Missing the other's face—
Literally and metaphorically
Missing the other's presence.

Poignant lines from the Psalmist
Give expression to this aspect
Of the divine-human relationship,
But there's a universality here that
Applies to all intimate relationships:

"How long, O Lord? Will you forget me
Forever? How long will you hide your face
From me?"[15] "'Come,' my heart says,
'Seek his face!' Your face Lord,
Do I seek. Do not hide your face...."[16]

It's a repeated plea in the Psalms:
"My soul longs for you, O God.
My soul thirsts . . . for the living God.
When shall I come
And behold the face of God?"[17]

"Hear my prayer, O Lord;
Let my cry come to you.
Do not hide your face from me
In the day of my distress.
Answer me . . . when I call."[18]

15. Ibid., Psalm 13:1.
16. Ibid., 27:8–9.
17. Ibid., 42:1b, 2b.
18. Ibid., 102:1–2.

One can understand these
Plaintive cries as calling
Upon God—from whom
The person feels estranged—
To be present as if seeing the face.

Then in the letters of Saint Paul
There is an almost ecstatic
Focus on God in one's heart,
Which he links to the incarnation,
And probably to his own conversion.

"For it is the God who said,
'Let light shine out of darkness,'
Who has shown in our hearts
To give the light of the knowledge
Of the glory of God

In the face of Jesus Christ."[19]
Paul links the Creation story—
Where we read that "darkness
Covered the face of the deep"
Until God says "Let there be light"—[20]

Paul links this emergence of light
With the shocking light which
Knocked him off his horse,
Blinded him, and—due to his
Inner encounter with Jesus—

19. Ibid., II Corinthians 4:6.
20. Ibid., Genesis 1:1–2.

Led to his transformation
Into a new creature![21]
This enlightenment gave him
An experiential knowledge and
Understanding of what God

Did and revealed in Jesus Christ:
God—more clearly than
Ever before—took on a
Human face! Jesus was
God's face, literally, yes,

But Jesus' whole being
Was the "face," the revealing,
The presence, the Way,
The Truth, the Life of God![22]
Astonishing really!

Paul's conversion experience
Helped him realize that Jesus—
All that God expressed and
Revealed of Godself in Jesus—
Can be present in any human heart;

That we can be—anyone can be—
The face of the Living God!
God alive within a person,
Revealing what God is about
Or not, depending on how we live.

If we choose to be the face of God,

21. Ibid., Acts 9:1–22.
22. Ibid., John 14:6.

Paul writes that we "are a letter
Of Christ, written not with ink,
But with the Spirit of the Living God,
Not on tablets of stone but

On tablets of human hearts."[23]
Paul writes ecstatically but carefully
About the development of intimacy
With God from the time of Moses
Until the appearance of Jesus.

He reminds us that Moses
Would put a veil over his face
After emerging from the tent
In which he spoke with
God face to face,

Because Moses' face shone
So brightly that people were afraid
To see Moses' unveiled face.
But God's presence in Jesus' face,
Paul says—and the experience

Of the Spirit of Jesus
Present and alive in one's heart—
Makes the veil unnecessary.
The Spirit alive within a person
Can be seen in the person's face.[24]

23. Ibid., II Corinthians 3:3.
24. Ibid., 3:7–17.

Playing with imagery to explain
This reality, as well as its
Edifying and sanctifying power,
Paul continues ecstatically:
"All of us with unveiled faces,

Seeing the glory of the Lord
As though reflected in a mirror,
Are being transformed
Into the same image [of God's
Face and presence in Jesus]

From one degree of glory
to another, for this comes
From the Lord, the Spirit."[25]
Since we don't see God's glory
In Jesus' literal human face,

It's reflected glory, as if
We're looking at God's presence
In our own faces or in
The faces of one another.
Astonishing! Think about it!

That's how present God is!
What's in a face, indeed.
So much more than
We can know,
Yet a manifestation

Of a person—a suggestion

25. Ibid., 3:18.

Of the life within.
Flashes of emotion
In a given moment;
At the same time a lifetime

Of a unique, individualized
Relative mix of joy and pain,
Disappointment and hope,
Peace and suffering, etched
In inimitable lines on a face.

Beauty is indeed then
Way more than skin deep.
All that a face presents,
Along with all that dwells
Behind it, revolutionizes

What began as beauty
Seen in one's mother's face,
Becomes beauty as a relationship
With a human embodiment
Of spiritual habitation;

Or lack thereof: desolation.
Mother comes and goes,
Hopefully is present enough
To enable the infant to
Establish object constancy—

An inner cognitive image

Which has been perceived often
Enough to become consolidated
And fixed in the infant's mind,
So that it can be called up

Even when mother is absent.
But absence can still be unsettling.
So, too, the Psalmist seeks—
In times of isolation,
Vulnerability, or suffering—

To invoke and reestablish inner
Connection with Divine Presence—
Which one knows is there
In spite of one's doubts and
Feelings of estrangement.

Presence and absence:
We're separate individuals
While also being
Relational creatures:
All of that is in a face.

At this deeper spiritual level
We may feel connected or
Disconnected from the Divine
Spirit living and breathing in us,
And we speak of this as

Feeling the presence or absence

Of the face of God, which then
Corresponds to the degree
To which we reflect, reveal
Or see in ourselves or one another,

The face of God.

Scriptural stories and texts,
And shared experiences of
Divine presence amongst members
Of one's spiritual family—
those who, as Jesus put it,

"Do the will of [the One]
Who sent me"—[26]help us
Achieve and maintain what
We might call "divine constancy":
Knowledge that God is present

Within us and around us
Whether we feel it or not
At any given time in our lives.
Jesus too felt forsaken
By God on the cross,[27]

But at the moment of his death,
Entrusted his spirit into God's hands.[28]
God who was present as Jesus

    26. Ibid., Mark 3:35.
    27. Ibid., 15:34.
    28. Ibid., Luke 23:46.

Throughout his human life
Assures us that whatever

A human being experiences—
From ecstasy to despair,
From hope to disillusionment,
from intimacy to abandonment,
From joy to rage or anger,

And whichever of these
Experiences is shown and
Seen on a human face—
Is not foreign to nor
Prohibitive of divine presence,

Nor evidence of a lack
Of divine presence.
Divine Spirit is present
In all that humans experience
And express—as Jesus' life,

Suffering, and death made clear.
Jesus experienced it all;
God was present in it all.
God is present in whatever
One sees in and on a face.

In this context, beauty
Transcends simple appearance,
And can become a profound awe
And love of every face

As created and loved by God.

One can then see any face—
Whether similar to one's own
Family or race or region or not—
As beautiful, as the living
Presence of God in a person!

---

* This poem was commissioned by my brother Ken while he and I spent an entire weekend discussing several of my other poems. Thanks, Ken!

MOONLIGHT GLIMMER

The moon was so bright that night
of the wild winter weather day
(that had dropped eight inches of snow,
followed by an inch of rained ice
then topped by a skiff more of snow)

that I noticed while looking out
my bedroom window a glint
or a glimmer of light
on the back side of
an ice-covered twig,

which because it was iced
looked like it was lit from within,
aglow and twinkling on the top
and bottom of the twig as well as
on the back side away from me.

I shifted my head a bit
to see if this could be.
I knew it was moonlit
but how could it be
that this pinpoint of light
from the faraway moon
on the back side of the twig
was twinkling right there
on that twig near me?

The world aglow with mystery:
light from the moon
playing with ice on a twig
thence reflected to my
fascinated eyes
on a cold winter night.

Bibliography

Arkema, Carroll E. "Goodbye to Dad." In *Poems of Mourning and Healing Memory*, 11–20. Eugene, OR: Resource Publications, 2017.

Beebe, Beatrice, and Frank Lachmann. *The Origins of Attachment: Infant Research and Adult Treatment*. Routledge, 2013.

Celani, David P. "Fairbairn's Structural Model and His Radical Approach to Psychoanalytic Treatment." In *Fairbairn's Object Relations Theory in the Clinical Setting*, 51–83. New York: Columbia University Press, 2010.

Freud, Sigmund. *The Ego and the Id*. New York: W. W. Norton & Company, Inc. 1960.

Hatch, Edwin. "Breath on Me, Breath of God." In *The Presbyterian Hymnal*, #316. Louisville, Kentucky: Westminster/John Knox, 1990.

The Holy Bible: New Revised Standard Version. Nashville/Burlingame: Thomas Nelson, 1990.

Spitz, Rene. *First Year of Life*. International Universities Press, 1966.

Winnicott, D. W. "Ego Distortion in Terms of True and False Self." In *The Maturational Processes and the Facilitating Environment: Studies in the Theory of Emotional Development*, 140–152. New York: International Universities Press, Inc., 1965.

www.ingramcontent.com/pod-product-compliance
Lightning Source LLC
Chambersburg PA
CBHW071418160426
43195CB00013B/1735